Trading For Beginners:

Mastering The Markets A Trader's Journey from Zero to Hero

Marcus Hill

Trading For Beginners

Summary

Trading For Beginners: 1
Mastering The Markets A Trader's Journey from Zero to Hero 1
Introduction 5
The Big, Bad World of Financial Markets 14
The Foundation of Smart Trading: Welcome to the Nerdy Side 26
Welcome to the Art Studio: The World of Technical Analysis 38
Finding Your Trading Style: The Buffet of Strategies 49
Day Trading Strategies: Speed Demons of the Market ... 49
Swing Trading Strategies: The Middle Ground 53
Position Trading Strategies: Playing the Long Game 56
Algorithmic Trading Strategies: Letting the Machines Do the Work 59
Risk Management within Strategies: Protecting Your Capital 61
Wrapping It Up 63
The Trader's Safety Net: Why Risk Management Is Non-Negotiable 65
Wrapping It Up 74
The Mind Game: Why Psychology Matters in Trading 76
Wrapping It Up 85
Welcome to the Future: An Introduction to Cryptocurrencies 86
Wrapping It Up 100
Stepping Up Your Game: Why Advanced Trading Concepts Matter 102
Wrapping It Up 114
The Journey from Novice to Pro: What It Takes to Build a Trading Career 115

Chapter 10: Trading Technology and Tools 126
The Evolution of Trading Technology 126
Essential Tools for Modern Traders 127
Algorithmic and Automated Trading 129
Leveraging Artificial Intelligence and Machine Learning
.... 132
Risk Management Tools 134
Emerging Technologies: Blockchain and Decentralized Finance (DeFi) 135
Integrating Technology into Your Trading Strategy 137
Wrapping It Up 139
Chapter 11: The Psychology of Successful Trading Communities 140
The Power of Trading Communities 140
Types of Trading Communities 141
Finding the Right Trading Community 144
Learning and Growing Through Community 146
Avoiding the Pitfalls of Groupthink 148
Building Your Own Trading Community 149
The Future of Trading Communities 151
Wrapping It Up 152
Conclusion: Recap and Final Thoughts 154
Recap of Key Concepts 154
Final Thoughts and Advice 157
The Road Ahead 158

Introduction

Meet Your Guide: An Unlikely Trading Guru

Welcome, future market maverick! My name is Max "The Bull" Harrington, but you can just call me Max. I wasn't always the slick, smooth-talking, market-wrangling trader you see before you (figuratively speaking). Nope, I started out like most of you—completely clueless, broke, and a little too eager to make a quick buck. In fact, my first "big trade" was betting $50 on a penny stock that tanked faster than my hopes of impressing my then-girlfriend. Spoiler alert: she's now married to some guy who sells insurance. But that's another story.

Over the years, I've learned the ins and outs of trading, often the hard way. From the late nights of pouring over charts that looked like an EKG machine on a bad day, to the euphoria of hitting that sweet, sweet profit, I've been through it all. And now, my friend, I'm here to share everything I've learned, along with some laughs, a few tears, and maybe a couple of shots of whiskey (optional, but recommended).

What You're Really Getting Into (And Why You Should Stick Around)

Let's get one thing straight right off the bat: trading is not easy money. If it were, I'd be writing this from my private island while sipping on a drink with an umbrella in it. The truth is, trading is a wild ride. It's exhilarating, frustrating, rewarding, and sometimes it makes you want to throw your laptop out the window. But it's also one of the most fulfilling things you can do if you're willing to put in the work.

In this book, I'm going to guide you through the often confusing, sometimes treacherous, but ultimately rewarding world of trading. By the time we're done, you'll be able to hold your own against the pros, or at the very least, impress your friends at parties by casually dropping terms like "Bollinger Bands" and "Fibonacci retracement." Trust me, nothing says cool like talking about market indicators over cocktails.

Here's a taste of what's coming your way:

- **Foundational Knowledge**: We'll start by breaking down the financial markets so they're less intimidating than your mother-in-law. You'll learn who's who, what's what, and why all those numbers on the screen matter.
- **Analytical Techniques**: Whether you're a numbers nerd or just trying to avoid losing your shirt, we'll cover both fundamental and technical analysis. I'll show you how to read charts like a pro, even if the last graph you looked at was your kid's growth chart.
- **Trading Strategies**: I've got strategies for every personality type—whether you're a thrill-seeker who loves day trading or a slow-and-steady swing trader. We'll get you set up with a plan that suits your style and doesn't make you lose sleep (or hair).

- **Risk Management**: If trading is like surfing, risk management is your life jacket. I'll teach you how not to drown in the market's choppy waters, and maybe even have some fun along the way.
- **Advanced Topics**: For those of you who like to live dangerously, we'll dive into options, futures, and forex. Don't worry, I'll hold your hand (metaphorically) and we'll get through it together.
- **Trading Psychology**: This is the part where I get to play armchair psychologist. We'll talk about why your brain is your own worst enemy when it comes to trading and how to outsmart yourself (and others).

Now, you might be wondering, "Who the heck is this Max guy, and why should I listen to him?" Good question. Besides having a stellar collection of Hawaiian shirts and a penchant for terrible puns, I've been trading for over a decade. I've seen markets soar, crash, and do weird things that even seasoned traders couldn't explain. Through it all, I've managed to make a decent living, have some fun, and avoid total financial ruin (so far). My goal is to help you do the same—minus the Hawaiian shirts, unless that's your thing.

Why This Book?

There are a ton of trading books out there, many of which are written by people who take themselves way too seriously. Don't get me wrong; trading is serious business, but that doesn't mean we can't have a little fun while we're at it. This book is different. I'm not just going to throw a bunch of jargon at you and expect you to figure it out. We're going to break things down, crack a few jokes, and maybe learn a thing or two about life along the way.

Here's the deal: I believe that learning should be enjoyable. If you're not having fun, you're not going to stick with it, and if you don't stick with it, you're not going to succeed. So, if you're ready to dive into the world of trading with a guide who's been there, done that, and lived to tell the tale (with a smile), then you're in the right place.

The Journey Ahead

I'm not going to sugarcoat it—trading is a journey, and it's not always an easy one. You'll have days where everything clicks, and you'll feel like the king (or queen) of Wall Street. And then you'll have days where you wonder why you ever thought this was a good idea. But that's okay. Every successful trader has been there. The key is to keep learning, keep practicing, and keep your sense of humor intact.

Over the course of this book, we're going to explore everything you need to know to become a successful trader. From the basics of how markets work to the intricacies of trading strategies, you'll get the full scoop. But I'm not just going to hand you a bunch of dry facts. I'll share my own experiences—the good, the bad, and the downright ugly—so you can learn from my mistakes and (hopefully) avoid making them yourself.

We'll start with the foundation—understanding financial markets. Don't worry, I promise to make it more interesting than watching paint dry. From there, we'll move on to the fun stuff: analysis, strategy, and, of course, making money. But remember, this isn't a get-rich-quick scheme. It's a journey, and like any good journey, it's going to have its ups and downs. The important thing is to enjoy the ride and learn as much as you can along the way.

Common Misconceptions and Realities

Before we get too deep into the nitty-gritty, let's clear up a few things. There are a lot of misconceptions out there about trading, and I'd hate for you to start this journey with stars in your eyes and dollar signs in your head—only to end up disappointed.

- **Trading is Easy Money**: If I had a dollar for every time someone told me trading was easy money, I wouldn't need to trade. The truth is, trading is a skill, and like any skill, it takes time to learn. Sure, you might get lucky on a trade or two, but relying on luck is a quick way to end up broke.
- **You Need a Ton of Cash to Start**: Here's the thing: you don't need to be a millionaire to start trading. In fact, you can start with a relatively small amount of money. The important thing is to manage that money wisely. Remember, it's not about how much you start with—it's about how smart you are with what you've got.
- **You Can Predict the Market**: If I could predict the market with 100% accuracy, I'd be writing this from my private jet. The reality is, nobody—no matter how experienced—can predict the market

perfectly. The key is to manage risk, make informed decisions, and not get too cocky when things are going well.
- **Trading is Just Like Gambling**: Okay, let's settle this once and for all. Trading is not gambling. Sure, there's risk involved, but trading is about making calculated decisions based on data, analysis, and experience. Gambling, on the other hand, is throwing money at chance and hoping for the best. If you're treating trading like a casino, you're doing it wrong.

The Mindset of a Successful Trader

Here's where I get all philosophical on you. Trading isn't just about numbers and charts—it's about mindset. If you want to succeed, you've got to get your head in the game. That means staying disciplined, being patient, and not letting your emotions run the show.

- **Discipline**: Think of discipline as your best friend in the trading world. It's what keeps you from making dumb decisions when you're tempted to go off-script. Stick to your plan, follow your rules, and don't let the market's mood swings mess with your head.
- **Patience**: Patience is a virtue, especially in trading. Sometimes, the best move is no move at all. Waiting for the right opportunity is better than jumping into a bad trade because you're bored or anxious. Remember, the market isn't going anywhere—it'll be there when you're ready.

- **Adaptability**: Markets change, and so should you. What worked yesterday might not work tomorrow. The key is to stay flexible, keep learning, and don't get too attached to any one strategy. Adaptability is what keeps you in the game when others are getting left behind.
- **Humor**: Yes, humor! If you can't laugh at yourself after a bad trade, you're going to have a rough time. Trading can be stressful, and if you take it too seriously, it's going to chew you up and spit you out. Learn to roll with the punches and find the humor in the ups and downs.

So, are you ready to dive into the wild world of trading with your new buddy Max? Good! Strap in, because it's going to be one heck of a ride. Just remember, trading is a journey, not a destination. And like any good journey, it's the experiences, lessons, and laughs along the way that make it worthwhile.

Conclusion

This introduction has given you a taste of what's to come, and I hope you're as excited as I am to get started. We've got a lot of ground to cover, but I promise to keep it entertaining, insightful, and maybe even a little bit life-changing (or at least, portfolio-changing).

In the next chapter, we'll start with the basics—understanding financial markets. I'll walk you through what makes the markets tick, who the major players are, and why you should care. Trust me, it's more interesting

Trading For Beginners

than it sounds. So grab your favorite beverage, get comfy, and let's get this show on the road!

Trading For Beginners

Chapter 1: Understanding Financial Markets

The Big, Bad World of Financial Markets

Alright, future trading tycoon, let's talk about the wild jungle that is the financial markets. Picture this: a massive, ever-changing ecosystem where the strong thrive, the weak get eaten alive, and everyone's trying to figure out where the heck they fit in. Sounds intense, right? Well, that's because it is. But don't worry—I've got your back, and by the end of this chapter, you'll have a solid understanding of what these markets are, how they work, and why they matter to you.

What Exactly Are Financial Markets?

Let's start with the basics: what the heck are financial markets, anyway? If you're picturing a bustling marketplace with traders shouting out prices like in those old movies, you're not too far off—just swap the physical market for digital screens and the shouting for rapid-fire typing, and you're basically there.

In a nutshell, financial markets are places where people buy and sell financial instruments—think stocks, bonds, commodities, currencies, and more. These markets are where companies, governments, and individuals come to raise money, invest, hedge risk, or, in some cases, just gamble (though we've already discussed how we're NOT here to gamble, right?).

Now, let's take a step back and look at why these markets exist in the first place. Imagine a world without financial markets. It would be like trying to trade a goat for a barrel of oil—super inconvenient, right? Financial markets provide the structure and infrastructure needed to facilitate trade, allowing companies to raise capital and investors to buy and sell assets efficiently. They're like the beating heart of the global economy, pumping money, resources, and opportunities through the system.

But here's where it gets fun. Financial markets aren't just boring, mechanical systems—they're living, breathing entities influenced by human emotions, global events, and even the latest tweet from a tech billionaire who shall remain nameless (you know who I'm talking about). This is what makes trading so fascinating and, at times, utterly bewildering.

The Different Species in the Market Jungle

Now that you know what financial markets are, let's meet the inhabitants. The market is teeming with all sorts of creatures, from the mighty institutional investors to the scrappy retail traders like you and me. Here's a quick rundown of the key players:

- **Institutional Investors**: These are the big fish in the market. We're talking about hedge funds, pension funds, mutual funds, and insurance companies. They have deep pockets and can move markets with their trades. Think of them as the lions of the jungle—majestic, powerful, and not to be messed with. When an institutional investor makes a move, the ripples can be felt across the market. Ever seen a lion take down a wildebeest? Yeah, it's kind of like that—except with less blood and more spreadsheets.

- **Retail Investors**: That's you! Retail investors are individuals who buy and sell securities for their personal accounts. We're the little guys, the underdogs, the ones who have to be smarter, quicker, and more adaptable to survive and thrive. But don't worry—underdogs have a way of pulling off some pretty impressive wins. Just think of David and Goliath, or that time your favorite underdog sports team actually won the championship. The moral? Never underestimate the power of a well-informed retail investor with a solid strategy.
- **Market Makers**: These are the folks who make sure there's always someone to trade with. Market makers provide liquidity by buying and selling securities, and they make their money on the spread—the difference between the bid (buy) and ask (sell) prices. Think of them as the busy bees of the market, always buzzing around to keep things flowing. Without market makers, trying to trade would be like trying to buy a hot dog at a baseball game with no vendors around—not gonna happen. They ensure that the gears of the market keep turning smoothly.
- **Brokers**: Brokers are the middlemen (and women) who facilitate trades between buyers and sellers. They're like your friendly neighborhood matchmakers, but instead of setting you up with a date, they're helping you buy that hot tech stock

or short that sluggish oil company. They make their money through commissions or fees. A good broker can be like a fairy godparent, helping you navigate the market and find the right opportunities. A bad broker, on the other hand, can be more like a used car salesman—so choose wisely.

- **Speculators**: These are the thrill-seekers of the market, the adrenaline junkies who are in it for the excitement and the potential for big profits. They don't necessarily care about the underlying value of what they're trading—they just want to ride the waves of market movements. Speculators are the surfers of the financial world, catching waves of volatility and hoping to come out on top. They add liquidity and volume to the markets, but they also bring a lot of risk. If you've ever seen a surfer wipe out on a massive wave, you know how quickly things can go south. But when they ride that perfect wave? Pure glory.

- **Governments and Central Banks**: These are the elephants in the room—big, powerful, and capable of causing massive shifts in the market with a single move. Governments issue bonds to finance their operations, and central banks (like the Federal Reserve in the U.S.) control monetary policy, which can have a huge impact on interest rates, inflation, and, by extension, the markets. When an elephant stomps, the ground shakes, and when a central bank makes a move, the markets pay attention. Imagine trying to have a picnic in the park when suddenly, an elephant charges through—yeah, it's kinda like that when the Fed decides to change interest rates.

Market Instruments: The Tools of the Trade

Alright, now that we've met the players, let's talk about the toys they play with—market instruments. These are the financial products that get bought and sold in the markets. There are a ton of different instruments out there, but here are the big ones you need to know about:

- **Stocks**: Stocks are shares of ownership in a company. When you buy a stock, you're essentially buying a small piece of that company. If the company does well, the value of your stock goes up, and you can sell it for a profit. If the company tanks... well, let's just say you won't be sending them a Christmas card. Stocks are like the bread and butter of trading—everyone's got them in their portfolio. They're also one of the most accessible and straightforward ways to get into the market. Think of stocks as your trusty bicycle—reliable, easy to use, and gets you where you need to go.
- **Bonds**: Bonds are a bit different. When you buy a bond, you're essentially lending money to a company or government, and in return, they promise to pay you back with interest. Bonds are generally considered safer than stocks, but they usually offer lower returns. Think of bonds as the sensible, responsible cousin who always wears a

seatbelt and never speeds. They're not as exciting as stocks, but they're reliable and steady, like that friend who always shows up on time and never forgets your birthday.

- **Commodities**: Commodities are physical goods like gold, oil, wheat, and coffee. Trading commodities can be a bit like riding a rollercoaster—prices can swing wildly based on supply and demand, geopolitical events, and even the weather. But for those who can stomach the ride, commodities can offer some serious profit potential. Imagine being a gold trader and waking up to news of a major geopolitical crisis—gold prices could skyrocket overnight, and if you were prepared, you'd be in a prime position to cash in. Just be careful not to spill your coffee when the markets go wild.
- **Currencies (Forex)**: The foreign exchange market, or forex, is where currencies are traded. This is the largest and most liquid market in the world—trillions of dollars change hands every day. Forex trading involves buying one currency while selling another, and traders make money by betting on changes in exchange rates. Forex is fast-paced and can be highly volatile, so it's not for the faint of heart. Imagine a high-speed chess match where the pieces move even when you're not looking—yeah, that's forex. If you thrive under pressure and love the thrill of fast decision-making, forex might just be your game.

- **Derivatives**: Derivatives are financial contracts whose value is derived from the performance of an underlying asset, like a stock, bond, or commodity. Common types of derivatives include options, futures, and swaps. These instruments can be used to hedge risk or to speculate, but they can also be complex and risky, so tread carefully. Think of derivatives like the spice rack in your kitchen—they can add flavor and excitement to your portfolio, but if you use too much, things can go south fast. Ever tried cooking with ghost peppers? Yeah, that's what over-leveraging derivatives can feel like.

Market Indices: The Pulse of the Market

Let's talk about market indices, which are basically the scoreboards of the financial world. They track the performance of a group of stocks, giving you a snapshot of how the market (or a particular segment of it) is doing. Here are some of the most important indices you'll need to know:

- **S&P 500**: This is the big one, folks. The S&P 500 tracks the performance of 500 of the largest publicly traded companies in the U.S. It's widely considered to be one of the best indicators of the overall health of the U.S. stock market. If the S&P 500 is up, people are generally feeling good about the economy. If it's down… well, maybe it's time to stock up on canned goods. The S&P 500 is like the thermometer of the market—when it's running hot, so is the economy; when it's cold, you might want to grab a blanket.

- **Dow Jones Industrial Average (DJIA)**: The Dow is one of the oldest and most well-known indices, tracking 30 large, publicly owned companies in the U.S. It's often used as a shorthand for how the market is doing, but keep in mind that it only represents a small slice of the market. The Dow is like that celebrity everyone knows—famous, influential, but doesn't necessarily represent the whole picture. It's good to know what the Dow's up to, but don't base all your decisions on it.
- **NASDAQ Composite**: This index is heavily weighted towards tech stocks, so if you're into companies like Apple, Google, and Tesla, the NASDAQ is your jam. It's also known for being more volatile than the S&P 500, which can mean bigger gains—or bigger losses. The NASDAQ is like the cool kid in school—innovative, always on the cutting edge, and sometimes a bit unpredictable. If you're trading tech stocks, keep a close eye on the NASDAQ—it'll give you a good sense of where the wind is blowing in the tech world.
- **Russell 2000**: The Russell 2000 tracks 2,000 small-cap companies in the U.S. It's a good indicator of how smaller companies are faring, and it can offer insights into the health of the broader economy, especially during times of economic recovery or growth. The Russell 2000 is like the underdog of the indices—plucky, full of potential, and often overlooked by the big players. But don't

underestimate it; small-cap stocks can pack a punch, especially when the economy is on the rise.
- **FTSE 100, Nikkei 225, and DAX**: These are the big indices outside of the U.S. The FTSE 100 represents the largest companies on the London Stock Exchange, the Nikkei 225 covers the top companies in Japan, and the DAX tracks the 30 major companies in Germany. If you're trading internationally, keep an eye on these. Think of them as your global weather report—what's happening in these markets can have ripple effects across the world, so it's good to stay informed.

Market indices are important because they give you a quick and easy way to gauge market sentiment. Are people bullish, bearish, or just plain confused? The indices will tell you. But remember, indices are just one piece of the puzzle. They give you the big picture, but you'll need to dig deeper to understand what's really going on in the markets.

Why Should You Care About All This?

Now, I know what you're thinking: "Max, this is all great, but why should I care about indices and market players and all this other stuff? I just want to make some money!" Fair question, my friend.

Understanding the structure of the financial markets and the role of different players and instruments is like learning the rules of the game before you start playing.

Imagine trying to play poker without knowing what a flush or a full house is—it wouldn't end well, would it? The same goes for trading. The more you understand about how the markets work, the better equipped you'll be to make smart, informed decisions.

Plus, having a solid grasp of market fundamentals gives you an edge over the competition. Remember, the markets are full of sharks, and the more knowledge you have, the less likely you are to end up as chum. Knowledge is power, and in the financial markets, it's the difference between sinking and swimming.

But there's another reason why you should care about all this: it's your money on the line. Whether you're trading to build wealth, achieve financial freedom, or just have a bit of fun, the stakes are real. By understanding the markets, you're not just playing the game—you're playing to win.

A Tale from the Trading Trenches

Let me share a little story from my early days of trading. Back when I was still wet behind the ears, I decided to dip my toes into the world of forex. I figured, "How hard can it be? It's just currency trading." Armed with my newfound confidence and a few online tutorials, I threw some money into a trade, betting that the U.S. dollar would rise against the euro.

At first, things were looking good. The dollar was inching up, and I was already picturing my future as a forex wizard. But then, out of nowhere, the European Central Bank made an announcement that sent the euro soaring and the dollar plummeting. In the blink of an eye, my "sure thing" trade turned into a nightmare.

I learned two valuable lessons that day: First, never underestimate the power of central banks (remember those elephants?). Second, always stay informed about what's happening in the markets—because if you don't, you could get trampled.

The moral of the story? The more you know about the markets and the forces that move them, the better equipped you'll be to navigate the ups and downs. And trust me, there will be plenty of both.

Wrapping It Up

So there you have it—your crash course in financial markets. We've covered what financial markets are, who the key players are, the different types of market instruments, and why market indices matter. If your head's spinning a bit, don't worry—that's normal. Take a deep breath, maybe grab a snack, and let it all sink in.

Remember, Rome wasn't built in a day, and neither are trading empires. This is just the beginning of your journey, and we've got plenty more ground to cover. In the next chapter, we'll dive into the nitty-gritty of **Fundamental Analysis**—how to dig into the numbers and figure out whether a company is worth your hard-earned cash or if it's better left alone. Trust me, you won't want to miss it.

Until then, keep those trading dreams alive and your sense of humor intact. The markets may be a jungle, but with the right knowledge, tools, and mindset, you can thrive in it. And hey, if nothing else, you'll at least have some great stories to tell at your next cocktail party.

Chapter 2: Fundamental Analysis

The Foundation of Smart Trading: Welcome to the Nerdy Side

Alright, folks, it's time to put on your detective hat and grab your magnifying glass because we're about to dive deep into the world of fundamental analysis. Now, I know what you're thinking: "Max, can't I just skip this part and jump straight to making money?" Trust me, I get it. Crunching numbers and analyzing balance sheets might not sound as thrilling as watching a stock price rocket to the moon. But here's the deal—fundamental analysis is like the secret sauce to trading success. It's what separates the wannabe traders from the ones who actually make it big.

In this chapter, we'll explore what fundamental analysis is, why it's important, and how you can use it to make smart trading decisions. We'll dig into economic indicators, financial statements, and even industry trends. By the time we're done, you'll be able to look at a company's financials and know whether it's a hidden gem or a sinking ship. So buckle up, because we're about to get nerdy—in the best possible way.

The Basics of Fundamental Analysis

First things first: what the heck is fundamental analysis, and why should you care? Simply put, fundamental analysis is the process of evaluating a company's financial health, performance, and growth potential to determine its true value. While technical analysis focuses on price movements and patterns, fundamental analysis digs into the "why" behind those movements.

Think of fundamental analysis as being like a mechanic inspecting a car before you buy it. Sure, the car might look shiny and new on the outside (that's the price), but what's under the hood? Is the engine in good shape? Are the brakes working? How about the transmission? Fundamental analysis helps you answer these questions for a company. It's about understanding the engine that drives the stock price—things like earnings, revenue, assets, and liabilities.

But here's the kicker: the market doesn't always price stocks accurately. Sometimes, a stock's price might be lower than its true value (making it a bargain), or it might be higher than it deserves to be (a bubble waiting to burst). Fundamental analysis helps you spot these discrepancies so you can buy low, sell high, and laugh all the way to the bank.

Understanding Economic Indicators

Before we dive into the nitty-gritty of company financials, let's zoom out and take a look at the bigger picture. You see, companies don't operate in a vacuum—they're part of the broader economy, and economic conditions can have a huge impact on their performance. That's where economic indicators come in.

Economic indicators are like the weather forecast for the economy. They give you insights into how the economy is doing and where it might be headed. Here are some of the key indicators you should keep an eye on:

- **Gross Domestic Product (GDP)**: GDP measures the total value of all goods and services produced in a country. It's like the scorecard for the economy—if GDP is growing, the economy is doing well. If it's shrinking, not so much. When GDP is on the rise, companies generally see higher sales and profits, which is good news for their stock prices. On the other hand, a declining GDP can signal tough times ahead.
- **Unemployment Rate**: The unemployment rate tells you how many people are out of work and actively looking for a job. A low unemployment rate is usually a sign of a healthy economy, where businesses are hiring and consumers have money to spend. But if unemployment is high, it can mean consumers are tightening their belts, which could hurt company earnings.
- **Inflation**: Inflation measures the rate at which prices for goods and services are rising. A little inflation is normal and even healthy, but if it gets out of control, it can erode purchasing power and lead to higher costs for businesses. Central banks, like the Federal Reserve, often adjust interest rates to keep inflation in check, and these changes can have a big impact on the markets.
- **Interest Rates**: Speaking of interest rates, these are set by central banks and influence the cost of borrowing money. Lower interest rates make borrowing cheaper, which can spur investment and spending—good for stocks. Higher rates, on the other hand, can slow down the economy and

make bonds more attractive than stocks, potentially leading to a market downturn.
- **Consumer Confidence Index (CCI)**: The CCI measures how optimistic or pessimistic consumers are about the economy. If consumers are confident, they're more likely to spend money, which boosts company revenues. If they're worried, they might cut back on spending, which can hurt businesses. It's like taking the temperature of the consumer's mood—if they're feeling good, that's usually a positive sign for the market.

These indicators are essential because they help you understand the economic environment in which companies operate. Even if a company is doing everything right, it can still be affected by broader economic trends. By keeping an eye on these indicators, you can get a sense of the "macro" picture and make more informed decisions about which stocks to buy or sell.

Analyzing Company Financials

Alright, now let's roll up our sleeves and get into the real meat of fundamental analysis: analyzing company financials. This is where you get to channel your inner Sherlock Holmes and dig into the numbers to figure out whether a company is worth your investment.

Every publicly traded company is required to publish financial statements, which provide a detailed look at their financial health. These statements include the income statement, balance sheet, and cash flow statement. Let's break them down:

- **Income Statement**: The income statement shows a company's revenues, expenses, and profits over a specific period (usually a quarter or a year). It's like a report card that tells you how well the company is doing in terms of generating money. Key metrics to look at include:
    - **Revenue**: This is the total amount of money the company brought in from its sales. Higher revenue is generally a good sign, but make sure to check if it's growing consistently or if there's a decline.
    - **Gross Profit**: Gross profit is the revenue minus the cost of goods sold (COGS). It shows how efficiently the company is producing its products or services.
    - **Net Income**: Net income is the company's profit after all expenses, taxes, and interest have been deducted. It's the bottom line—literally—and a key indicator of profitability.
    - **Earnings Per Share (EPS)**: EPS is the portion of a company's profit allocated to each outstanding share of stock. It's a good way to measure profitability on a per-share basis, which makes it easier to compare companies of different sizes.
- **Balance Sheet**: The balance sheet provides a snapshot of a company's assets, liabilities, and

shareholders' equity at a specific point in time. It's like a financial x-ray that shows you what the company owns and owes. Key metrics to examine include:

- **Assets**: These are the resources owned by the company, such as cash, inventory, property, and equipment. Assets are divided into current (short-term) and non-current (long-term) assets.
- **Liabilities**: Liabilities are the company's debts and obligations, such as loans, accounts payable, and bonds. Like assets, liabilities are divided into current (short-term) and non-current (long-term) liabilities.
- **Shareholders' Equity**: This represents the owners' claim on the company's assets after all liabilities have been paid. It's calculated as assets minus liabilities and is often referred to as the company's "net worth."

- **Cash Flow Statement**: The cash flow statement shows how much cash is flowing in and out of the company over a specific period. It's divided into three sections: operating activities, investing activities, and financing activities. Cash flow is crucial because it shows whether the company has enough cash to cover its expenses and invest in growth. Here's what to look for:
  - **Operating Cash Flow**: This is the cash generated from the company's core

business operations. Positive operating cash flow is a good sign that the company's business model is working.
- **Investing Cash Flow**: This section shows cash spent on investments, such as purchasing equipment or acquiring other businesses. While negative cash flow in this area might seem bad, it can actually be a positive sign if the company is investing in growth.
- **Financing Cash Flow**: This includes cash from issuing or repurchasing shares, borrowing money, or paying dividends. It tells you how the company is managing its capital structure.

Key Ratios and Metrics

Now that you know how to read financial statements, let's talk about some of the key ratios and metrics that can help you assess a company's financial health. These ratios are like the "vital signs" of a company, giving you quick insights into its performance.

- **Price-to-Earnings Ratio (P/E Ratio)**: The P/E ratio is one of the most commonly used metrics in fundamental analysis. It's calculated by dividing the stock price by the earnings per share (EPS). The P/E ratio tells you how much investors are willing to pay for each dollar of earnings. A high P/E ratio might indicate that the stock is overvalued, while a low P/E ratio could mean it's undervalued. But be careful—context matters. A high P/E might be justified if the company has strong growth prospects, and a low P/E could signal underlying problems.

- **Return on Equity (ROE)**: ROE measures how effectively a company is using its equity to generate profits. It's calculated by dividing net income by shareholders' equity. A high ROE indicates that the company is generating good returns on the money invested by shareholders. It's like the return on investment for the company's owners—higher is generally better.
- **Debt-to-Equity Ratio**: This ratio compares a company's total liabilities to its shareholders' equity. It's a measure of financial leverage, showing how much debt the company is using to finance its operations. A high debt-to-equity ratio can be a red flag, indicating that the company might be overleveraged and at risk of financial distress. On the flip side, a low ratio suggests a more conservative approach, which might be appealing to risk-averse investors.
- **Current Ratio**: The current ratio measures a company's ability to pay its short-term liabilities with its short-term assets. It's calculated by dividing current assets by current liabilities. A current ratio greater than 1 indicates that the company has more short-term assets than liabilities, which is a sign of good liquidity. However, a ratio that's too high could mean the company is not efficiently using its assets.

- **Dividend Yield**: If you're investing in dividend-paying stocks, the dividend yield is an important metric to consider. It's calculated by dividing the annual dividend by the stock price. The dividend yield tells you how much return you're getting in the form of dividends relative to the stock price. A high dividend yield can be attractive to income-focused investors, but be sure to check if the dividend is sustainable.

Industry and Sector Analysis

Alright, you've got a handle on the company's financials—now it's time to zoom out a bit and look at the bigger picture: the industry and sector the company operates in. Just like a fish is influenced by the water it swims in, a company's performance is affected by the broader industry and sector trends.

- **Industry Analysis**: An industry is a group of companies that produce similar products or services. For example, the tech industry includes companies like Apple, Microsoft, and Google, while the energy industry includes ExxonMobil, Chevron, and BP. When analyzing an industry, consider factors like the overall demand for the industry's products, the level of competition, and any regulatory or technological changes that could impact the industry. For example, the rise of electric vehicles is a major trend affecting the automotive industry, while the shift to renewable energy is shaking up the energy industry.

- **Sector Analysis**: A sector is a broader category that includes multiple industries. For example, the technology sector includes industries like software, hardware, and semiconductors, while the healthcare sector includes pharmaceuticals, biotechnology, and medical devices. Sector analysis helps you understand the broader economic forces that are impacting a group of related industries. For example, an economic recession might hit the consumer discretionary sector hard (think retail, travel, and entertainment), while the healthcare sector might be more resilient.

When analyzing a company, it's important to consider how it compares to its industry peers and how the broader sector is performing. Even a well-run company can struggle if its industry is in decline, and a rising tide in a strong sector can lift even weaker companies.

Applying Fundamental Analysis to Different Markets

By now, you're probably feeling pretty confident about your ability to analyze companies. But here's the thing—fundamental analysis isn't just for stocks. It can be applied to other markets as well, like bonds, commodities, and even cryptocurrencies (we'll get to that in a later chapter). Let's take a quick look at how fundamental analysis can be adapted for different markets:

- **Bonds**: When analyzing bonds, you'll want to focus on the issuer's creditworthiness, which is a measure of their ability to repay the bond. This involves looking at financial metrics like the debt-to-equity ratio, interest coverage ratio (which measures how easily the issuer can pay interest on its debt), and the issuer's credit rating. You'll also want to consider macroeconomic factors like interest rates and inflation, which can affect bond prices.

- **Commodities**: For commodities like gold, oil, or wheat, fundamental analysis involves looking at supply and demand factors. For example, oil prices might be influenced by geopolitical events in major oil-producing countries, changes in production levels by OPEC, or advances in alternative energy sources. Weather patterns can impact agricultural commodities like wheat or corn. Understanding these factors can help you predict price movements.
- **Currencies**: In the forex market, fundamental analysis involves looking at the economic health of the countries whose currencies you're trading. This includes analyzing economic indicators like GDP, unemployment rates, and inflation, as well as central bank policies and geopolitical events. For example, if the U.S. Federal Reserve raises interest rates, the U.S. dollar might strengthen relative to other currencies.

Wrapping It Up

Whew! That was a lot to cover, but congratulations—you've just completed your crash course in fundamental analysis. By now, you should have a solid understanding of how to analyze a company's financial health, evaluate economic indicators, and consider industry and sector trends. You're well on your way to becoming a savvy, informed trader who makes decisions based on data, not just gut feelings.

In the next chapter, we're going to switch gears and dive into **Technical Analysis**—how to read charts, spot patterns, and use indicators to predict price movements. If fundamental analysis is the science of trading, then technical analysis is the art. And trust me, it's going to be just as fun.

Until then, keep those spreadsheets handy and remember: knowledge is your most valuable asset in the trading world. The more you understand about the markets and the companies you're investing in, the better your chances of success. And who knows? With a little bit of luck and a lot of hard work, you might just find yourself riding the next big wave to financial freedom.

Chapter 3: Technical Analysis

Welcome to the Art Studio: The World of Technical Analysis

So, you've got a solid grasp of fundamental analysis—you can read a balance sheet like a pro and know your way around a financial statement. But now it's time to channel your inner artist and step into the colorful, often mystifying world of technical analysis. If fundamental analysis is about understanding a company's worth, technical analysis is about understanding market psychology. It's the study of price movements, patterns, and trends—essentially, the science of predicting the unpredictable.

But don't worry, this isn't some kind of black magic (though sometimes it can feel like it). Technical analysis is built on centuries of market data, human behavior, and a bit of probability theory. In this chapter, we'll explore how to read charts, identify key patterns, and use various indicators to make informed trading decisions. Whether you're a visual learner who loves charts or someone who just wants to know when to buy and sell, this chapter is for you.

The Basics of Technical Analysis

Let's kick things off with the basics: what exactly is technical analysis, and why should you care? In simple terms, technical analysis is the study of historical price data to predict future price movements. It's based on the idea that history tends to repeat itself—especially in the markets, where human emotions like fear and greed often drive prices.

While fundamental analysis looks at the intrinsic value of a stock, technical analysis focuses purely on price and volume. It doesn't care why a stock is moving; it only cares that it is moving. Technical analysts, also known as chartists, believe that all the information you need to make trading decisions is already baked into the price. In other words, "the chart tells all."

Now, before you roll your eyes and think this is just some elaborate form of tea leaf reading, consider this: some of the world's most successful traders, including legends like Paul Tudor Jones and Bruce Kovner, have relied heavily on technical analysis. So, while it might seem a bit abstract at first, it's a skill worth mastering.

Chart Types: The Canvas of Technical Analysis

Let's start with the bread and butter of technical analysis—charts. Just like an artist has different canvases to choose from, traders have different types of charts. Each type has its own strengths and is suited for different kinds of analysis. Here are the three main types you'll encounter:

- **Line Charts**: The simplest and most straightforward of all charts, the line chart connects the closing prices of a security over a specified period with a line. It's great for getting a quick overview of the overall trend. If you're the type who likes to keep things simple, the line chart might be your best friend. Just don't expect it to give you all the intricate details—it's more of a "big picture" kind of tool.

- **Bar Charts**: Bar charts provide more information than line charts, showing the opening, closing, high, and low prices for each time period. Each bar represents one period of trading (e.g., a day, an hour, a minute), with the top of the bar showing the highest price, the bottom showing the lowest, and little horizontal lines on the left and right showing the open and close, respectively. Bar charts are like the Swiss Army knife of charts—they give you a lot of information in a compact format, making them useful for more detailed analysis.
- **Candlestick Charts**: Ah, the beloved candlestick chart—arguably the most popular type of chart among traders. Originating in Japan over a century ago, candlestick charts provide the same information as bar charts (open, close, high, and low), but they're visually easier to interpret. Each "candlestick" has a body (representing the range between the open and close) and wicks (or shadows) that show the high and low prices. If the close is higher than the open, the body is usually green or white; if the close is lower than the open, the body is red or black. Candlestick charts are like the comic books of trading—colorful, expressive, and full of hidden stories.

Candlestick charts, in particular, are the go-to for many traders because they provide a wealth of information at a glance. Once you get the hang of reading them, you'll start to see patterns that can give you insights into market sentiment.

Chart Patterns: Decoding the Market's Secret Language

Charts are great, but what really makes them powerful are the patterns that emerge over time. These patterns are like the market's secret language, giving you clues about what might happen next. Here are some of the most important patterns you'll want to familiarize yourself with:

- **Head and Shoulders**: The head and shoulders pattern is one of the most reliable reversal patterns in technical analysis. It consists of three peaks: a higher peak (the "head") between two lower peaks (the "shoulders"). When you see this pattern, it often signals that an uptrend is coming to an end and that a downtrend might be on the horizon. Think of it like a mountaintop—after reaching the peak (the head), it's usually downhill from there.
- **Double Tops and Bottoms**: These patterns are also reversal signals. A double top looks like the letter "M" and occurs after an uptrend, indicating that the price might be about to fall. A double bottom, on the other hand, looks like a "W" and happens after a downtrend, suggesting that the price might be about to rise. It's like the market

trying to find its balance before deciding which direction to go next.

- **Triangles**: Triangles are continuation patterns that indicate the market is consolidating before continuing in the direction of the trend. There are three types of triangles: ascending (bullish), descending (bearish), and symmetrical (neutral). Ascending triangles have a flat top and rising bottoms, descending triangles have a flat bottom and falling tops, and symmetrical triangles have converging trendlines. Think of triangles as the market catching its breath before the next big move.
- **Flags and Pennants**: These are also continuation patterns, usually indicating a brief pause in a strong trend. Flags are rectangular shapes that slope against the prevailing trend, while pennants are small symmetrical triangles. Both patterns suggest that the trend will continue once the pattern is complete. It's like the market taking a quick pit stop before getting back on the road.
- **Cup and Handle**: This bullish continuation pattern looks like a tea cup, with the "cup" forming a rounded bottom and the "handle" forming a small consolidation before the price breaks out. It's a sign that the market is gearing up for another leg higher. Just like your morning coffee, a cup and handle pattern can give the market a fresh burst of energy.

Learning to recognize these patterns takes time and practice, but once you do, you'll have a powerful tool at your disposal. Just remember, no pattern is foolproof—always combine pattern analysis with other tools for confirmation.

Indicators and Oscillators: Your Trading Companions

Now that you've got a handle on charts and patterns, it's time to introduce you to some of your new best friends: indicators and oscillators. These tools help you analyze price data in more detail, giving you insights that might not be immediately visible on the chart. Here are some of the most popular ones:

- **Moving Averages**: Moving averages smooth out price data to help you identify the direction of the trend. There are two main types: simple moving averages (SMA), which calculate the average price over a set period, and exponential moving averages (EMA), which give more weight to recent prices. Moving averages are like the GPS of trading—they help you figure out where the market is heading.
- **Relative Strength Index (RSI)**: The RSI is an oscillator that measures the speed and change of price movements. It ranges from 0 to 100 and is used to identify overbought or oversold conditions. An RSI above 70 suggests the market is overbought and might be due for a pullback, while an RSI below 30 indicates it's oversold and might be due for a bounce. Think of RSI as the market's

mood ring—it tells you whether the market is feeling a little too optimistic or overly pessimistic.

- **Moving Average Convergence Divergence (MACD)**: The MACD is a trend-following indicator that shows the relationship between two moving averages (usually the 12-day and 26-day EMAs). When the MACD line crosses above the signal line (a 9-day EMA of the MACD), it's a bullish signal; when it crosses below, it's bearish. The MACD histogram, which shows the difference between the MACD line and the signal line, can also give you clues about the strength of the trend. MACD is like your market weathervane—it helps you gauge the direction and momentum of the trend.
- **Bollinger Bands**: Bollinger Bands consist of a moving average and two standard deviation lines plotted above and below it. They expand and contract based on market volatility, helping you identify overbought or oversold conditions. When prices touch the upper band, the market might be overbought; when they touch the lower band, it might be oversold. Bollinger Bands are like your market guardrails—they keep you on track and help you avoid driving off a cliff.
- **Stochastic Oscillator**: The stochastic oscillator compares a security's closing price to its price range over a specified period. It ranges from 0 to 100, with readings above 80 indicating overbought conditions and readings below 20 indicating oversold conditions. The stochastic oscillator is like a speedometer for the market—

helping you see if the market is moving too fast and might need to slow down.

Indicators and oscillators are incredibly useful, but they're most powerful when used in combination. For example, you might use moving averages to identify the trend, RSI to gauge momentum, and Bollinger Bands to spot potential reversal points. The key is to find a combination of tools that works for you and helps you make more informed trading decisions.

Support and Resistance: The Market's Invisible Barriers

One of the most important concepts in technical analysis is support and resistance. These are price levels where the market has historically had trouble moving past. Understanding these levels can help you make better decisions about when to enter or exit a trade.

- **Support**: Support is a price level where a stock tends to find buying interest, causing the price to "bounce" upward. It's like the floor under the price—a level where buyers step in and prevent it from falling further. If a stock drops to a support level and holds, it might be a good buying opportunity.
- **Resistance**: Resistance is the opposite of support—it's a price level where a stock tends to find selling pressure, causing the price to "bounce" downward. It's like the ceiling above the price—a level where sellers step in and prevent it from rising further. If a stock rises to a resistance

level and fails to break through, it might be a good time to sell or short.

These levels aren't always exact—they're more like zones where the market has a history of reversing direction. When a support level is broken, it can turn into resistance, and when a resistance level is broken, it can turn into support. This phenomenon is known as a "breakout" and can signal the start of a new trend.

Understanding support and resistance is crucial because it helps you identify key price levels where the market might change direction. It's like knowing the market's pressure points—hit the right spot, and you can trigger a profitable move.

Advanced Technical Analysis Techniques

If you're still with me, congratulations—you've made it through the fundamentals of technical analysis! But if you're hungry for more, let's dive into some advanced techniques that can give you an extra edge in the market.

- **Fibonacci Retracement**: Fibonacci retracement is a tool used to identify potential support and resistance levels based on the Fibonacci sequence—a mathematical pattern found in nature. Traders use it to predict how far a market might pull back before continuing in the direction of the trend. The key levels to watch are 38.2%, 50%, and 61.8%. It's like bringing a ruler to the market, helping you measure the potential depth of a pullback.

- **Ichimoku Cloud**: The Ichimoku Cloud is a complex indicator that shows support and resistance levels, trend direction, and momentum all in one. It consists of five lines that create a "cloud" on the chart. If the price is above the cloud, it's bullish; if it's below, it's bearish. The Ichimoku Cloud is like the Swiss Army knife of indicators—versatile, powerful, and able to do a lot of things at once.
- **Elliott Wave Theory**: Elliott Wave Theory is based on the idea that market prices move in predictable cycles, known as waves. These waves are driven by investor psychology and follow a specific pattern of five waves in the direction of the trend, followed by three corrective waves. While it can be complex, Elliott Wave Theory can help you identify the bigger picture and predict long-term market movements. It's like learning to read the market's mind—tricky, but powerful if you get it right.
- **Volume Analysis**: Volume analysis involves looking at the amount of trading activity to confirm trends and predict reversals. For example, if a stock breaks out to a new high on high volume, it's more likely to continue rising than if the breakout happens on low volume. Volume is like the market's megaphone—it amplifies the signals and tells you how much conviction there is behind a move.

Wrapping It Up

Congratulations, you've just completed a deep dive into the world of technical analysis! By now, you should have a solid understanding of how to read charts, identify key patterns, and use indicators to make informed trading decisions. Whether you're day trading, swing trading, or just trying to time your investments better, these tools and techniques will help you navigate the markets with more confidence.

In the next chapter, we're going to dive into **In-Depth Trading Strategies**—this is where we'll take everything you've learned so far and apply it to real-world trading scenarios. We'll cover day trading, swing trading, position trading, and more. It's going to be a deep dive, so bring your snorkel and let's get ready to make some waves!

Until then, keep those charts handy and remember: the market may be unpredictable, but with the right tools and mindset, you can turn uncertainty into opportunity.

Chapter 4: In-Depth Trading Strategies

Finding Your Trading Style: The Buffet of Strategies

By now, you've got a good grasp of the tools at your disposal—charts, indicators, patterns, and a solid understanding of how to analyze the markets. But here's the thing: knowing how to analyze the markets is one thing; knowing how to trade them is another. That's where trading strategies come in.

Think of trading strategies like a buffet. There's a little something for everyone, whether you're into the fast-paced action of day trading, the more relaxed pace of swing trading, or the long game of position trading. The key is to find the strategies that suit your personality, risk tolerance, and goals. In this chapter, we're going to explore a variety of strategies in depth, so you can pick and choose the ones that work best for you.

Day Trading Strategies: Speed Demons of the Market

Day trading is all about making quick moves. It's like the Formula 1 of trading—fast, intense, and not for the faint of heart. Day traders buy and sell securities within the same trading day, aiming to capitalize on short-term price movements. Here are some of the most popular day trading strategies:

Scalping: Quick Profits in Fast Markets

Scalping is the ultimate hit-and-run strategy. Scalpers aim to make small profits on a large number of trades, often holding positions for just a few seconds or minutes. The idea is to take advantage of tiny price movements, and the key to success is speed and precision. Here's how it works:

- **Entry and Exit**: Scalpers use real-time charts, often with one-minute intervals, to identify small price movements. They typically enter and exit trades quickly, sometimes within seconds, to lock in profits before the market can reverse.
- **Volume**: Scalping requires a high volume of trades to be profitable. Since the profit on each trade is small, you need to make a lot of trades to add up to significant gains. This means finding highly liquid markets where you can enter and exit positions quickly without slippage.
- **Risk Management**: Since scalping involves a lot of trades, it's crucial to manage your risk carefully. Scalpers often use tight stop-loss orders to limit potential losses, and they focus on maintaining a high win rate to offset the small profits per trade.

Scalping is perfect for traders who thrive on quick decisions and can handle the pressure of fast-paced markets. It's not for everyone, but if you've got the nerves of steel and the reflexes of a cat, scalping might be your ticket to consistent profits.

Momentum Trading: Riding the Wave

Momentum trading is all about riding the wave of market momentum. Momentum traders look for stocks that are moving strongly in one direction, either up or down, and aim to jump on board for the ride. The key is to get in while the momentum is strong and get out before it fades. Here's the playbook:

- **Identifying Momentum**: Momentum traders use technical indicators like moving averages, RSI, and MACD to identify stocks with strong momentum. They look for stocks that are making new highs or lows, breaking out of consolidation patterns, or showing strong volume.
- **Entry Points**: The best time to enter a momentum trade is when the stock has just broken out and the momentum is starting to build. Look for confirmation from volume—if the stock is moving on high volume, it's a good sign that the momentum is strong.
- **Exit Points**: The challenge with momentum trading is knowing when to get out. The key is to exit while the momentum is still strong but before it reverses. Some traders use trailing stop-loss orders to lock in profits as the stock continues to move in their favor.

Momentum trading is ideal for traders who like to go with the flow and are good at spotting trends as they develop. It requires quick thinking and the ability to act decisively when the market moves.

Range Trading: Capitalizing on Market Movement

Range trading is all about identifying stocks that are trading within a specific range and buying at the lower end of the range (support) while selling at the upper end (resistance). It's a more measured approach than momentum trading and works best in markets that aren't trending strongly in one direction. Here's how to make it work:

- **Identifying Ranges**: The first step in range trading is to identify stocks that are trading within a well-defined range. This is usually done using horizontal support and resistance lines on a chart. A stock that bounces between these levels repeatedly is a prime candidate for range trading.
- **Entry Points**: Buy at support and sell at resistance. It sounds simple, but timing is crucial. You want to enter the trade as close to the support level as possible to maximize your potential profit. Look for confirmation signals like a bounce off the support level or a reversal candlestick pattern.
- **Exit Points**: Sell at resistance or if the stock breaks below support. If the stock approaches the resistance level, consider selling to lock in your gains. If the stock breaks below the support level, it could be a sign that the range is about to end, and you might want to exit to avoid losses.

Range trading is a great strategy for traders who prefer a more methodical approach and don't want to chase the fast-moving markets. It works best in markets that are moving sideways, with no clear trend in either direction.

Swing Trading Strategies: The Middle Ground

Swing trading sits between day trading and position trading. It's like the marathon of trading—not too fast, not too slow, but just right. Swing traders hold positions for several days or weeks, aiming to capture medium-term price movements. Here are some popular swing trading strategies:

Trend Following: The Power of Persistence

Trend following is one of the most popular swing trading strategies. The idea is simple: identify the direction of the trend and trade in that direction. If the trend is up, you buy; if the trend is down, you sell. The key to success is staying with the trend for as long as possible. Here's how it works:

- **Identifying the Trend**: Use tools like moving averages, trendlines, and the ADX indicator to identify the direction of the trend. A rising moving average or a series of higher highs and higher lows is a sign of an uptrend. A falling moving average or lower highs and lower lows indicates a downtrend.
- **Entry Points**: Enter the trade when the trend is confirmed, usually after a pullback or consolidation. For an uptrend, buy when the stock pulls back to a support level or the moving average and then starts to rise again. For a downtrend, sell when the stock rallies to a resistance level or moving average and then starts to fall.

- **Exit Points**: Stay in the trade as long as the trend remains intact. Use trailing stop-loss orders to lock in profits as the trend progresses. If the trend shows signs of reversing, like breaking a key support or resistance level, it's time to exit.

Trend following is ideal for traders who have the patience to stay in a trade for several days or weeks and who are comfortable with holding positions overnight. It's a strategy that can yield significant profits if you catch a strong trend early.

Countertrend Trading: Going Against the Flow

Countertrend trading is the opposite of trend following. Instead of trading with the trend, countertrend traders look for opportunities to trade against it. The idea is to buy when the market is overextended to the downside and sell when it's overextended to the upside. It's a contrarian strategy that requires a good understanding of market psychology. Here's how to do it:

- **Identifying Overextension**: Look for signs that the market is overbought or oversold, such as extreme RSI readings, Bollinger Bands, or a parabolic move in the price. These signals suggest that the trend might be due for a reversal.
- **Entry Points**: Enter the trade when the market shows signs of reversing. For example, if the market is in a strong downtrend and RSI falls below 30, it might be a good time to buy. Conversely, if the market is in a strong uptrend and RSI rises above 70, it might be time to sell.

- **Exit Points**: Countertrend trades are usually short-term, so it's important to exit quickly once the reversal happens. Set tight stop-loss orders to protect against the possibility that the trend will continue, and take profits as soon as the market moves in your favor.

Countertrend trading is for traders who like to go against the crowd and are good at spotting when the market has gone too far, too fast. It's a higher-risk strategy, but it can be highly rewarding if executed correctly.

Breakout Trading: Catching Market Moves Early

Breakout trading is all about catching a big move early. Breakouts occur when a stock moves beyond a key support or resistance level, often on high volume. These moves can lead to significant price changes, and the goal of breakout trading is to capture as much of that move as possible. Here's how to do it:

- **Identifying Breakouts**: Look for stocks that are approaching a key support or resistance level with increasing volume. A consolidation pattern like a triangle, flag, or pennant can also indicate that a breakout is imminent.
- **Entry Points**: Enter the trade when the stock breaks above resistance (for a bullish breakout) or below support (for a bearish breakout). Make sure to confirm the breakout with volume—higher volume suggests that the breakout is more likely to succeed.

- **Exit Points**: Set a profit target based on the size of the previous trading range or use a trailing stop to capture as much of the move as possible. If the breakout fails and the stock falls back into the trading range, exit the trade to avoid losses.

Breakout trading is ideal for traders who want to catch big moves early and are comfortable with a bit of volatility. It's a strategy that can lead to significant profits if you're quick to act when the breakout occurs.

Position Trading Strategies: Playing the Long Game

Position trading is the most laid-back of all the trading styles. It's like the slow-cooked barbecue of trading—you're in it for the long haul, letting your trades simmer and develop over weeks, months, or even years. Position traders focus on the big picture, aiming to capture the majority of a trend. Here are some key position trading strategies:

Long-Term Trends: Playing the Big Picture

Long-term trend following is the bread and butter of position trading. The idea is to identify a major trend and ride it for as long as possible, capturing the bulk of the move. This strategy requires patience and a strong understanding of market cycles. Here's how it works:

- **Identifying Long-Term Trends**: Use weekly and monthly charts to identify long-term trends. Look for stocks that are in a clear uptrend or

downtrend, with a series of higher highs and higher lows (uptrend) or lower highs and lower lows (downtrend).
- **Entry Points**: Enter the trade when the trend is confirmed, usually after a pullback or consolidation. For an uptrend, buy on a dip to a key support level or moving average. For a downtrend, sell on a rally to a key resistance level.
- **Exit Points**: Stay in the trade as long as the trend remains intact. Use long-term moving averages or trendlines to guide your exits. If the stock breaks below a major support level or moving average, it might be time to exit.

Long-term trend following is perfect for traders who are patient and willing to hold positions for months or even years. It's a strategy that can yield substantial profits if you catch a major trend early.

Fundamental-Driven Trading: Investing with a Trading Edge

Fundamental-driven trading combines the principles of investing with the techniques of trading. It's about finding fundamentally strong companies and holding them for the long term, but also using technical analysis to time your entries and exits. Here's how to approach it:

- **Identifying Strong Fundamentals**: Use fundamental analysis to identify companies with strong earnings growth, solid balance sheets, and competitive advantages. Look for companies that

are leaders in their industry and have a history of strong performance.
- **Entry Points**: Use technical analysis to time your entry. Buy when the stock is in an uptrend and has just pulled back to a support level or moving average. This helps you get in at a good price while the fundamentals are still strong.
- **Exit Points**: Hold the stock as long as the fundamentals remain strong and the trend is intact. Use technical analysis to guide your exit—if the stock breaks below a key support level or shows signs of a trend reversal, it might be time to sell.

Fundamental-driven trading is ideal for traders who want to combine the best of both worlds—long-term investing and short-term trading. It's a strategy that requires a deep understanding of both fundamental and technical analysis, but it can be highly rewarding.

Dividend Capture: Profiting from Income Stocks

Dividend capture is a strategy that focuses on stocks that pay regular dividends. The idea is to buy the stock just before the dividend is paid and then sell it shortly after, capturing the dividend payment without holding the stock for the long term. Here's how to do it:

- **Identifying Dividend Stocks**: Look for stocks with a history of paying regular dividends and a high dividend yield. Dividend capture works best with stocks that have relatively stable prices and low volatility.

- **Entry Points**: Buy the stock just before the ex-dividend date, which is the date by which you must own the stock to receive the dividend. Make sure to account for transaction costs, as these can eat into your profits.
- **Exit Points**: Sell the stock shortly after the dividend is paid, ideally once the stock price has recovered from the typical post-dividend drop. If the stock is still in an uptrend, you might consider holding it for a bit longer to capture additional gains.

Dividend capture is a low-risk strategy that can provide a steady income stream, especially in a low-interest-rate environment. It's perfect for traders who prefer a more conservative approach and are looking for consistent returns.

Algorithmic Trading Strategies: Letting the Machines Do the Work

In today's markets, algorithms aren't just for Google—they're also for traders. Algorithmic trading involves using computer programs to execute trades based on predefined criteria. It's like having a robot do your trading for you, with the goal of executing trades faster and more efficiently than a human could. Here are some popular algorithmic trading strategies:

High-Frequency Trading: Speed as a Strategy

High-frequency trading (HFT) is all about speed. HFT firms use sophisticated algorithms to execute a large number of trades in fractions of a second, often taking advantage of small price discrepancies in the market. Here's a glimpse into the world of HFT:

- **Strategy**: HFT strategies often involve arbitrage, where the algorithm exploits tiny price differences between different markets or assets. For example, the algorithm might buy a stock on one exchange and simultaneously sell it on another where the price is slightly higher.
- **Technology**: HFT requires cutting-edge technology, including low-latency trading platforms, direct market access, and colocated servers near the exchanges. The goal is to minimize the time it takes for the algorithm to execute trades.
- **Risk Management**: Since HFT involves a large number of trades, risk management is crucial. HFT firms use sophisticated risk models to monitor their positions in real-time and automatically exit trades if they exceed predefined risk limits.

High-frequency trading is a highly specialized strategy that requires significant resources and technical expertise. It's not something most individual traders can do, but it's a fascinating part of the modern trading landscape.

Quantitative Analysis: Using Data to Drive Decisions

Quantitative analysis, or "quant" trading, involves using mathematical models and statistical techniques to make trading decisions. Quant traders rely on data and algorithms to identify trading opportunities and execute trades. Here's how it works:

- **Strategy Development**: Quant traders develop strategies based on historical data and statistical models. These strategies are often backtested on historical data to ensure they would have been profitable in the past.
- **Execution**: Once a strategy is developed and tested, it's implemented using an algorithm that automatically executes trades based on the predefined criteria. The algorithm can monitor multiple markets simultaneously and execute trades in real-time.
- **Risk Management**: Quants use sophisticated risk management techniques, including value-at-risk (VaR) models, to monitor and manage their exposure. The goal is to maximize returns while keeping risk within acceptable limits.

Quant trading is ideal for traders with a strong background in mathematics, statistics, or computer science. It's a data-driven approach that requires significant technical expertise, but it can be highly profitable if done correctly.

Risk Management within Strategies: Protecting Your Capital

No matter what trading strategy you choose, risk management is crucial. It's the safety net that protects your capital and ensures that you can stay in the game for the long haul. Here's how to incorporate risk management into your trading strategies:

Tailoring Strategies to Risk Tolerance

Every trader has a different risk tolerance, and it's important to choose strategies that align with yours. If you're a conservative trader, you might prefer strategies like dividend capture or long-term trend following. If you're more aggressive, you might gravitate toward day trading or momentum trading. The key is to find a balance between risk and reward that you're comfortable with.

Setting Stop-Losses and Take-Profits

One of the most effective risk management tools is the stop-loss order, which automatically exits a trade if the price moves against you by a certain amount. Setting a stop-loss ensures that you limit your losses and protect your capital. Similarly, a take-profit order allows you to lock in profits when the price reaches a certain level.

- **Stop-Loss Orders**: Place your stop-loss at a level where the market would need to prove your trade wrong. For example, if you're buying a stock based on a support level, place your stop-loss just below that level.
- **Take-Profit Orders**: Set your take-profit at a level where you've reached your profit target, based on

the size of the previous trading range or the next resistance level.

By using stop-loss and take-profit orders, you can manage your risk more effectively and ensure that you're taking profits when they're available.

Backtesting and Strategy Refinement

Finally, it's important to backtest your strategies on historical data before implementing them in live trading. Backtesting allows you to see how your strategy would have performed in the past and identify any weaknesses. Once you've backtested your strategy, you can refine it by adjusting the parameters and rules to improve its performance.

- **Backtesting Tools**: Use trading platforms that offer backtesting capabilities to test your strategies on historical data. Look for platforms that provide a detailed analysis of your strategy's performance, including metrics like win rate, drawdown, and risk-adjusted returns.
- **Continuous Improvement**: Even after you've started trading with a strategy, it's important to continue refining it. Markets change, and what works today might not work tomorrow. By continuously monitoring and improving your strategies, you can stay ahead of the curve.

Wrapping It Up

Congratulations, you've just completed an in-depth exploration of trading strategies! By now, you should have a solid understanding of the various strategies available, from day trading to position trading to algorithmic trading. You've learned how to tailor these strategies to your risk tolerance, how to manage risk effectively, and how to continuously refine your approach.

In the next chapter, we'll dive into **Risk Management**—the cornerstone of successful trading. We'll explore how to protect your capital, manage your emotions, and develop a disciplined approach to trading. This is where the rubber meets the road, and it's a chapter you won't want to miss.

Until then, take some time to think about which strategies resonate with you and start developing a plan that fits your goals and risk tolerance. Remember, the best traders aren't necessarily the ones who make the most trades—they're the ones who make the smartest trades.

Chapter 5: Risk Management

The Trader's Safety Net: Why Risk Management Is Non-Negotiable

If there's one thing you take away from this book, let it be this: risk management is the foundation of successful trading. I don't care how brilliant your strategy is or how confident you are in your next big move—if you don't manage your risk, you're setting yourself up for a fall. Imagine being a tightrope walker without a safety net. Sure, the thrill is there, but one slip, and it's game over. In trading, your safety net is risk management, and in this chapter, we're going to make sure it's strong enough to catch you if you slip.

The Importance of Risk Management

Let's start with the basics: why is risk management so important? The answer is simple—it's about survival. Trading is inherently risky, and no strategy, no matter how well-researched or meticulously planned, is foolproof. The markets can be unpredictable, volatile, and downright nasty at times. Without proper risk management, even a single bad trade can wipe out months (or years) of hard-earned gains.

But risk management isn't just about avoiding disaster. It's also about ensuring that your trading is sustainable over the long term. By controlling your risk, you give yourself the chance to stay in the game, learn from your mistakes, and capitalize on opportunities when they arise. It's the difference between being a flash in the pan and becoming a seasoned, successful trader.

Position Sizing: The Goldilocks Principle of Trading

One of the most important aspects of risk management is position sizing—deciding how much of your capital to allocate to each trade. Position sizing is like the Goldilocks principle: too big, and you're risking too much; too small, and you're not maximizing your potential returns. You want to find that "just right" size that balances risk and reward.

So, how do you determine the right position size? Here's a step-by-step guide:

- **Determine Your Risk Tolerance**: Start by deciding how much of your capital you're willing to risk on a single trade. A common rule of thumb is to risk no more than 1-2% of your total trading capital on any one trade. This means that if you have $10,000 in your trading account, you shouldn't risk more than $100 to $200 on a single trade.
- **Calculate the Distance to Your Stop-Loss**: Next, determine where you'll place your stop-loss order—the price level at which you'll exit the trade to prevent further losses. Calculate the difference between your entry price and the stop-loss price. This is the amount you're risking per share or contract.
- **Determine Position Size**: Finally, divide the amount of capital you're willing to risk by the amount you're risking per share or contract. The

result is the number of shares or contracts you should trade. For example, if you're willing to risk $200 and your stop-loss is $2 away from your entry price, you should trade 100 shares ($200 ÷ $2 = 100 shares).

Position sizing is crucial because it ensures that you're not putting all your eggs in one basket. By limiting your risk on each trade, you protect your capital from catastrophic losses and give yourself the chance to live to trade another day.

Setting Stop-Losses and Take-Profits: Your Trading Insurance

If position sizing is the Goldilocks principle, stop-losses are your insurance policy. A stop-loss order automatically exits your trade if the price moves against you by a certain amount. It's like having a safety mechanism that kicks in when things go wrong, ensuring that your losses are limited.

Here's how to use stop-losses effectively:

- **Technical Stop-Losses**: Place your stop-loss based on technical analysis. For example, if you're buying a stock because it's bouncing off a support level, place your stop-loss just below that support. If the price falls below that level, it's a sign that the support has failed, and you should exit the trade.
- **Volatility-Based Stop-Losses**: Another approach is to base your stop-loss on the stock's volatility.

More volatile stocks require wider stop-losses to avoid being stopped out by normal price fluctuations. You can use indicators like the Average True Range (ATR) to measure volatility and set your stop-loss accordingly.

- **Percentage Stop-Losses**: Some traders prefer to set their stop-loss as a fixed percentage of the entry price. For example, you might decide to exit the trade if the price moves 5% against you. This approach is simple but doesn't take into account the stock's unique characteristics or the market environment.
- **Trailing Stop-Losses**: A trailing stop-loss moves with the price as it advances in your favor, locking in profits along the way. For example, if you set a trailing stop-loss 5% below the market price, it will rise as the price rises, but if the price falls 5%, it will trigger an exit. Trailing stops are great for capturing profits in trending markets.

On the flip side, take-profit orders allow you to lock in gains when the price reaches a certain level. While it might be tempting to let your winners run indefinitely, there's a risk that the market could reverse, erasing your gains. Take-profit orders help you avoid this by securing profits at predefined levels.

Managing Emotions: The Psychology of Risk

If there's one thing that trips up traders more than anything else, it's emotions. Fear, greed, hope, and regret can all cloud your judgment and lead to impulsive decisions that hurt your bottom line. Managing your emotions is just as important as managing your trades, and it's a key component of risk management.

Here are some tips for keeping your emotions in check:

- **Stick to Your Plan**: The best way to manage emotions is to have a solid trading plan and stick to it. Your plan should include your entry and exit criteria, position sizing rules, and risk management strategies. By following your plan, you take the emotion out of trading and make decisions based on logic and analysis.
- **Accept Losses as Part of the Game**: No trader wins all the time. Losses are an inevitable part of trading, and the sooner you accept that, the better. Instead of dwelling on your losses, focus on learning from them and improving your strategy.
- **Avoid Overtrading**: Overtrading is a common mistake that's often driven by emotions like greed or the desire to "make back" losses. It's important to be patient and wait for high-quality setups that meet your criteria. Trading for the sake of trading is a surefire way to lose money.
- **Take Breaks**: If you find yourself getting frustrated, anxious, or overly excited, take a break. Step away from the screen, go for a walk, or do something that relaxes you. Clearing your head can help you return to the market with a fresh perspective.

- **Use Technology Wisely**: Consider using automated trading systems or alerts to help manage your trades and emotions. For example, if you have trouble sticking to your stop-losses, you can set up automatic stop-loss orders that will execute without your intervention.

Managing your emotions is a skill that takes time to develop, but it's essential for long-term success in trading. The more you can stay calm and disciplined, the better your decisions will be.

Diversification: Don't Put All Your Eggs in One Basket

Diversification is a key risk management strategy that involves spreading your capital across multiple assets, sectors, or markets. The idea is to reduce your exposure to any single investment, so that if one trade goes south, it won't take your entire portfolio with it.

Here's how to diversify effectively:

- **Asset Diversification**: Invest in a mix of different asset classes, such as stocks, bonds, commodities, and currencies. Different assets often respond differently to market conditions, so a diversified portfolio can help smooth out your returns.
- **Sector Diversification**: Even within the stock market, it's important to diversify across different sectors. For example, you might invest in technology, healthcare, finance, and consumer goods stocks, rather than putting all your money

into one sector. This reduces the risk that a downturn in one sector will wipe out your gains.
- **Geographic Diversification**: Don't limit your investments to just one country or region. Consider investing in international markets to spread your risk. Different countries have different economic cycles, and geographic diversification can help you benefit from growth in multiple regions.
- **Time Diversification**: Spread out your trades over time rather than making them all at once. This helps you avoid the risk of entering the market at the wrong time and gives you the flexibility to adjust your strategy as conditions change.

Diversification is often described as the only free lunch in investing. By spreading your risk across different assets and markets, you can reduce the impact of any single loss and improve your chances of long-term success.

The 1% Rule: A Simple, Effective Risk Management Strategy

If you're looking for a straightforward way to manage risk, the 1% rule is a great place to start. The rule is simple: never risk more than 1% of your total trading capital on a single trade. This means that if you have $10,000 in your trading account, you should risk no more than $100 on any one trade.

Here's why the 1% rule is so effective:

- **Limits Losses**: By capping your risk at 1% per trade, you limit the potential damage of any single loss. Even if you have a string of losing trades, your account won't be wiped out.
- **Promotes Discipline**: The 1% rule encourages you to be selective about the trades you take. Since your risk is limited, you'll be more likely to wait for high-quality setups that meet your criteria.
- **Reduces Emotional Impact**: Losing a small percentage of your account is much less emotionally taxing than losing a large chunk. The 1% rule helps you stay calm and focused, even when trades don't go your way.
- **Allows for Recovery**: With the 1% rule, even if you experience a drawdown, you can recover more easily. Since your losses are small, it takes fewer winning trades to get back to where you started.

The 1% rule is a simple but powerful way to manage risk, especially for new traders. It helps you protect your capital, stay disciplined, and build a solid foundation for long-term success.

Risk-Reward Ratio: Finding the Balance

Another important concept in risk management is the risk-reward ratio, which measures the potential profit of a trade relative to its potential loss. The goal is to find trades where the potential reward outweighs the potential risk, ideally by at least 2:1 or 3:1.

Here's how to calculate the risk-reward ratio:

- **Identify Your Stop-Loss Level**: Determine the price at which you'll exit the trade if it moves against you. The difference between your entry price and the stop-loss level is your risk per share or contract.
- **Identify Your Profit Target**: Determine the price at which you'll take profits if the trade moves in your favor. The difference between your entry price and the profit target is your potential reward per share or contract.
- **Calculate the Ratio**: Divide the potential reward by the potential risk to find the risk-reward ratio. For example, if you're risking $100 and your profit target is $300, the risk-reward ratio is 3:1.

A high risk-reward ratio means that you don't need to be right all the time to make money. Even if only half of your trades are successful, a 3:1 risk-reward ratio will still result in a profitable strategy. The key is to focus on trades where the potential reward justifies the risk.

Continuous Learning: The Key to Long-Term Success

Finally, risk management isn't just about specific strategies—it's also about continuous learning and improvement. The markets are constantly changing, and what works today might not work tomorrow. To stay ahead of the curve, you need to be committed to learning, adapting, and refining your approach.

Here are some ways to keep learning and improving:

- **Review Your Trades**: After each trade, take the time to review what went well and what didn't. Did you follow your plan? Did you manage your risk effectively? What could you do differently next time? Reviewing your trades helps you learn from your mistakes and build on your successes.
- **Stay Informed**: Keep up with market news, trends, and developments. Read books, attend webinars, and follow experienced traders to stay informed and inspired. The more you know, the better equipped you'll be to manage risk and make informed decisions.
- **Adapt to Market Conditions**: Markets go through different phases—bull markets, bear markets, high volatility, low volatility—and each phase requires a different approach. Be willing to adapt your strategies to suit the current market environment.
- **Invest in Your Education**: Consider taking courses or working with a mentor to deepen your understanding of trading and risk management. Investing in your education is one of the best ways to protect your capital and improve your long-term success.

Wrapping It Up

Risk management might not be the most glamorous part of trading, but it's undoubtedly the most important. By managing your risk effectively, you protect your capital, stay in the game, and give yourself the best chance of long-term success. Whether it's through position sizing, stop-losses, diversification, or continuous learning, every trader needs a solid risk management plan.

In the next chapter, we'll explore **Trading Psychology**—the mental side of trading that's just as crucial as the technical side. We'll dive into the emotions that can trip you up and how to develop the discipline and mindset needed to succeed in the markets. This is where the rubber meets the road, and it's a chapter you won't want to miss.

Until then, take some time to review your current risk management strategies and make any necessary adjustments. Remember, trading is a marathon, not a sprint, and the better you manage your risk, the farther you'll go.

Chapter 6: Trading Psychology

The Mind Game: Why Psychology Matters in Trading

Let's get one thing straight: trading is as much a mental game as it is a numbers game. You can have the best strategy in the world, but if you can't keep your emotions in check, you're going to have a hard time making it in the markets. Think of trading like a high-stakes poker game—you need skill, yes, but you also need nerves of steel and the ability to stay calm under pressure. In this chapter, we're going to explore the psychological side of trading and how you can develop the mental toughness needed to succeed.

The Psychology of a Trader: Know Thyself

Before we dive into specific strategies for managing your emotions, it's important to understand the psychological landscape of trading. At its core, trading is a test of your ability to manage uncertainty, control your impulses, and make decisions under pressure. Here are some of the key psychological challenges traders face:

- **Fear**: Fear is one of the most powerful emotions in trading, and it can manifest in many ways—fear of losing money, fear of missing out (FOMO), or even fear of pulling the trigger on a trade. Fear can cause you to hesitate, exit trades too early, or avoid taking risks altogether. The key to overcoming fear is to recognize it for what it is—

an emotional response to uncertainty—and to develop strategies for managing it.
- **Greed**: If fear is the devil on one shoulder, greed is the devil on the other. Greed can lead you to take unnecessary risks, chase after "sure things," or hold onto winning trades for too long in the hope of squeezing out a little more profit. Greed is driven by the desire for more, and if left unchecked, it can lead to devastating losses. The antidote to greed is discipline and the ability to stick to your trading plan.
- **Overconfidence**: There's nothing wrong with being confident in your abilities, but overconfidence can be dangerous in trading. It can cause you to take bigger risks than you should, ignore warning signs, or think you've "cracked the code" of the market. The markets have a way of humbling even the most experienced traders, so it's important to stay grounded and always be prepared for the unexpected.
- **Regret**: Regret is a common emotion in trading— whether it's regret over a missed opportunity, a trade gone wrong, or a decision made in the heat of the moment. Regret can lead to overtrading, revenge trading, or second-guessing your decisions. The key to overcoming regret is to accept that no trader is perfect and that every trade is a learning opportunity.
- **Hope**: Hope is a double-edged sword in trading. On one hand, it can keep you motivated and

focused on your goals. On the other hand, it can lead you to hold onto losing trades, hoping they'll turn around, or to take unnecessary risks in the hope of a big payoff. Hope is not a strategy—successful traders rely on analysis, discipline, and risk management to guide their decisions.

Understanding these emotions and how they influence your trading decisions is the first step to mastering the psychology of trading. The next step is developing the mental discipline to manage these emotions effectively.

Developing Mental Discipline: The Trader's Edge

Discipline is the cornerstone of successful trading. It's what allows you to stick to your plan, manage your risk, and keep your emotions in check. But let's be honest—discipline is easier said than done, especially when you're in the thick of the market and emotions are running high. Here are some strategies for developing the mental discipline needed to succeed in trading:

- **Create a Detailed Trading Plan**: Your trading plan is your roadmap—it outlines your strategy, risk management rules, entry and exit criteria, and more. But a plan is only effective if you follow it. Make sure your plan is detailed and realistic, and then commit to following it to the letter. When you're tempted to deviate from your plan, remind yourself why you created it in the first place.
- **Set Clear Goals**: Having clear, specific goals gives you something to strive for and helps keep you focused. Your goals should be realistic and

achievable—whether it's a certain percentage return on your portfolio, a target number of successful trades, or simply following your trading plan consistently. Break your goals down into smaller, actionable steps, and track your progress regularly.

- **Practice Patience**: Patience is a virtue in trading, and it's one of the hardest things to master. The markets don't always move on your schedule, and sometimes the best move is no move at all. Learn to wait for high-quality setups that meet your criteria, rather than jumping into trades out of impatience or boredom. Remember, trading is a marathon, not a sprint.
- **Use Visualization Techniques**: Visualization is a powerful tool that athletes and performers use to prepare for competition—and it can be just as effective in trading. Spend a few minutes each day visualizing yourself making calm, confident trading decisions, sticking to your plan, and managing your emotions effectively. This mental rehearsal can help you build confidence and reinforce positive behaviors.
- **Develop a Routine**: A consistent routine can help you stay disciplined and focused. This might include regular times for market analysis, trading, reviewing your performance, and even taking breaks. A routine helps create structure and reduces the chances of impulsive decisions. Just like an athlete has a pre-game routine, your

trading routine should prepare you mentally and emotionally for the trading day.
- **Practice Mindfulness**: Mindfulness involves staying present and aware of your thoughts, feelings, and surroundings without judgment. In trading, mindfulness can help you stay focused on the task at hand and avoid being swept away by emotions. Techniques like deep breathing, meditation, or simply taking a few moments to clear your mind can help you stay centered and make more rational decisions.

Mental discipline is a skill that takes time to develop, but it's one of the most valuable assets a trader can have. The more disciplined you are, the more consistent your results will be, and the better equipped you'll be to handle the challenges of the market.

Dealing with Losses and Drawdowns: Bouncing Back Stronger

Let's face it—losses are part of the trading game. No matter how skilled or experienced you are, there will be times when the market goes against you. The key to long-term success isn't avoiding losses altogether (because that's impossible); it's learning how to manage them and bounce back stronger.

Here's how to deal with losses and drawdowns effectively:

- **Accept Losses as Inevitable**: The first step to dealing with losses is to accept that they're a normal part of trading. Every trader, no matter how successful, experiences losses. What separates successful traders from the rest is their ability to accept losses without letting them affect their mindset or decision-making. Remember, it's not the individual trade that matters—it's the overall performance of your trading strategy.

- **Keep Losses in Perspective**: It's easy to get discouraged after a losing trade, but it's important to keep things in perspective. A single loss doesn't define your trading career, and it's unlikely to have a significant impact on your long-term performance—especially if you're managing your risk effectively. Keep your focus on the bigger picture and remember that trading is a long-term game.
- **Learn from Your Losses**: Every loss is an opportunity to learn and improve. After each losing trade, take the time to analyze what went wrong. Did you deviate from your plan? Was there something you missed in your analysis? Or was it simply a case of bad luck? By understanding the reasons behind your losses, you can make adjustments and avoid repeating the same mistakes in the future.
- **Avoid Revenge Trading**: Revenge trading is the urge to make up for a loss by immediately entering another trade, often with more risk. It's driven by the desire to "get back" at the market, but it almost always leads to more losses. If you find yourself wanting to jump back into the market after a loss, take a step back and wait until

you're calm and clear-headed before making your next move.

- **Manage Drawdowns with Discipline**: A drawdown is a period when your trading account experiences a series of losses, leading to a decline in your overall capital. Drawdowns are inevitable, but how you handle them is crucial. During a drawdown, it's important to stick to your risk management rules, avoid taking on more risk to "make back" losses, and consider reducing your position sizes until you regain your confidence.
- **Focus on Process, Not Outcomes**: One of the best ways to deal with losses is to focus on your process rather than the outcome of individual trades. If you followed your trading plan, managed your risk, and made rational decisions, then you've done everything right—even if the trade didn't work out. Over time, a disciplined process will lead to positive results.
- **Take Breaks When Needed**: If you're going through a tough period of losses, it's okay to take a break from trading. Stepping away from the markets for a few days or even weeks can help you clear your mind, regain perspective, and come back with renewed focus and energy.

Dealing with losses and drawdowns is one of the most challenging aspects of trading, but it's also one of the most important. By learning how to manage losses effectively, you'll be better equipped to handle the ups and downs of the market and build a successful trading career.

Building Confidence as a Trader: The Power of Positive Reinforcement

Confidence is a key ingredient in successful trading. Without confidence, it's difficult to pull the trigger on trades, stick to your plan, or manage your emotions effectively. But here's the thing—confidence isn't something you're born with; it's something you build over time through experience, practice, and positive reinforcement.

Here are some strategies for building and maintaining confidence as a trader:

- **Celebrate Your Wins**: It's important to acknowledge and celebrate your successes, no matter how small. Each winning trade is a testament to your skill, discipline, and hard work, and recognizing these wins helps reinforce positive behavior. Keep a journal of your successful trades and review it regularly to remind yourself of what you're capable of.
- **Review Your Progress**: Take the time to regularly review your overall trading performance. Look at your win rate, average profit and loss, and other key metrics. Seeing consistent progress, even if it's slow, can boost your confidence and motivate you to keep going.
- **Focus on What You Can Control**: In trading, there are many things you can't control—market

movements, news events, and other external factors. But there are also many things you can control, like your trading plan, risk management, and mindset. By focusing on what you can control, you'll feel more empowered and confident in your decisions.

- **Use Visualization and Affirmations**: Visualization and affirmations are powerful tools for building confidence. Spend a few minutes each day visualizing yourself as a successful, confident trader. Use positive affirmations like "I am a disciplined trader" or "I make rational, informed decisions" to reinforce a positive mindset.
- **Seek Feedback and Mentorship**: Sometimes, it's hard to see your own progress or identify areas for improvement. Seeking feedback from more experienced traders or working with a mentor can help you gain new insights, build confidence, and accelerate your development.
- **Focus on Consistency**: Confidence comes from knowing that you can replicate your success. Instead of trying to hit home runs with every trade, focus on being consistent. Aim for steady, incremental gains rather than big wins, and over time, your confidence will grow as you see the results of your efforts.

Confidence is something that builds over time, and it's a crucial component of long-term success in trading. By focusing on your process, celebrating your wins, and continuously improving, you'll develop the confidence you need to navigate the markets with poise and discipline.

Wrapping It Up

Trading psychology is often the missing piece in many traders' journeys. While strategies, analysis, and risk management are all important, it's your mindset and emotions that ultimately determine your success. By understanding the psychological challenges of trading and developing the mental discipline to manage your emotions, you'll be better equipped to navigate the markets and achieve your goals.

In the next chapter, we'll dive into **The Wild World of Cryptocurrency Trading**—a market that's as volatile as it is exciting. We'll explore the unique challenges and opportunities of trading cryptocurrencies, as well as the strategies you can use to profit from this emerging market. If you've ever been curious about Bitcoin, Ethereum, or the countless other digital currencies out there, you won't want to miss this chapter.

Until then, take some time to reflect on your own trading psychology. What emotions tend to trip you up? How can you develop more discipline and confidence in your trading? Remember, the mind is a powerful tool—use it wisely, and it will serve you well in your trading journey.

Chapter 7: The Wild World of Cryptocurrency Trading

Welcome to the Future: An Introduction to Cryptocurrencies

Alright, folks, buckle up, because we're about to dive into one of the most exciting and volatile markets out there—cryptocurrencies. If you've been around the financial block, you've probably heard of Bitcoin, Ethereum, and maybe even Dogecoin (thanks, Elon). But beyond the headlines and hype, there's a whole world of digital assets that's transforming the financial landscape and creating new opportunities for traders.

Cryptocurrencies are digital or virtual currencies that use cryptography for security. Unlike traditional currencies, which are issued by central banks, cryptocurrencies operate on decentralized networks based on blockchain technology. This means they're not controlled by any government or institution, making them a truly global and borderless form of money.

But let's not kid ourselves—cryptocurrencies are also notoriously volatile. Prices can skyrocket one day and plummet the next, making it a market that's as thrilling as it is risky. In this chapter, we're going to explore the ins and outs of cryptocurrency trading, from the basics of how these digital assets work to advanced strategies for capitalizing on their price movements.

The Evolution of the Crypto Market: From Bitcoin to DeFi

The story of cryptocurrencies begins with Bitcoin, the first and most well-known digital currency. Launched in 2009 by an anonymous person (or group) known as Satoshi Nakamoto, Bitcoin was created as a decentralized alternative to traditional money. Its underlying technology, blockchain, is a distributed ledger that records all transactions across a network of computers, ensuring transparency and security.

Bitcoin's success paved the way for thousands of other cryptocurrencies, each with its own unique features and use cases. Some, like Ethereum, introduced smart contracts—self-executing contracts with the terms of the agreement directly written into code. Others, like Ripple (XRP), focused on improving cross-border payments.

In recent years, we've seen the rise of decentralized finance (DeFi), a movement that aims to recreate traditional financial services—like lending, borrowing, and trading—on decentralized platforms using cryptocurrencies. DeFi has exploded in popularity, with billions of dollars now locked in DeFi protocols, creating new opportunities (and risks) for traders.

As the cryptocurrency market has evolved, so too have the strategies for trading these digital assets. Whether you're interested in day trading, swing trading, or long-term investing, the crypto market offers a range of opportunities for traders with the right knowledge and approach.

Key Cryptocurrencies: Bitcoin, Ethereum, and the Altcoin Army

Before we dive into specific trading strategies, it's important to understand the key players in the cryptocurrency market. While there are thousands of cryptocurrencies out there, not all of them are worth your attention. Let's start with the heavyweights:

- **Bitcoin (BTC)**: The original cryptocurrency, Bitcoin remains the most valuable and widely recognized digital asset. Often referred to as "digital gold," Bitcoin is seen by many as a store of value and a hedge against inflation. Its market dominance and liquidity make it a cornerstone of the cryptocurrency market.
- **Ethereum (ETH)**: Ethereum is the second-largest cryptocurrency by market capitalization and the leading platform for decentralized applications (dApps) and smart contracts. Unlike Bitcoin, which is primarily used as a currency or store of value, Ethereum is more like a global computing platform, enabling developers to build and deploy decentralized applications.
- **Ripple (XRP)**: Ripple is a digital payment protocol that aims to facilitate fast and low-cost international money transfers. While XRP, its native cryptocurrency, is used as a bridge currency in these transactions, Ripple's main focus is on providing a more efficient alternative to traditional cross-border payment systems.
- **Litecoin (LTC)**: Often referred to as the "silver to Bitcoin's gold," Litecoin is a peer-to-peer cryptocurrency that offers faster transaction times and lower fees than Bitcoin. It's similar to Bitcoin

in many ways but aims to be a more practical option for everyday transactions.

- **Cardano (ADA)**: Cardano is a blockchain platform that aims to provide a more secure and scalable infrastructure for the development of decentralized applications and smart contracts. It's known for its academic approach, with a strong focus on research and peer-reviewed development.
- **Polkadot (DOT)**: Polkadot is a multi-chain blockchain platform that enables different blockchains to interoperate with each other. Its goal is to create a more connected and scalable ecosystem of blockchains, with a focus on security and interoperability.
- **Dogecoin (DOGE)**: Originally created as a joke, Dogecoin has become a cultural phenomenon, thanks in part to its strong community and high-profile endorsements. While it started as a meme, Dogecoin has seen significant price increases, making it a popular choice for speculative traders.

These are just a few of the many cryptocurrencies you'll encounter in the market. Beyond the top players, there's a vast array of altcoins (alternative coins) with varying degrees of risk and potential. Some are innovative projects with strong use cases, while others are speculative ventures with little more than hype behind them. As with any market, it's important to do your research and understand the assets you're trading.

Understanding Blockchain and Its Impact on Trading

At the heart of every cryptocurrency is blockchain technology—a decentralized, distributed ledger that records transactions across a network of computers. Understanding how blockchain works is key to understanding the unique nature of cryptocurrencies and the opportunities and challenges they present for traders.

- **Decentralization**: One of the key features of blockchain is decentralization. Unlike traditional financial systems, where transactions are processed and verified by a central authority (like a bank), blockchain transactions are validated by a network of computers (known as nodes). This decentralization makes blockchain resistant to censorship and fraud, as there's no single point of failure.
- **Transparency**: Every transaction on a blockchain is recorded on a public ledger that can be viewed by anyone. This transparency ensures that all transactions are verifiable and can't be altered or tampered with after the fact. For traders, this means you can easily track the movement of assets and ensure that your transactions are secure.
- **Security**: Blockchain uses advanced cryptographic techniques to secure transactions and prevent unauthorized access. Each block in the chain is linked to the previous one through a cryptographic hash, creating a secure and immutable record of all transactions. This high level of security is one of the reasons why

blockchain is considered a revolutionary technology for financial services.
- **Smart Contracts**: On platforms like Ethereum, blockchain technology enables the creation of smart contracts—self-executing contracts with the terms of the agreement directly written into code. Smart contracts can automate a wide range of financial transactions, from simple transfers of value to complex decentralized finance (DeFi) applications.

Understanding the basics of blockchain technology is crucial for anyone looking to trade cryptocurrencies. It's what makes these assets unique and sets them apart from traditional financial instruments.

Unique Aspects of Crypto Trading: Volatility, Liquidity, and Security

Cryptocurrency trading comes with its own set of challenges and opportunities. While the potential for profit is high, so too is the risk. Here are some of the key factors that make crypto trading different from trading traditional assets:

- **Volatility**: Cryptocurrencies are known for their extreme price volatility. It's not uncommon for a cryptocurrency to see double-digit percentage swings in a single day—or even within a few hours. This volatility creates opportunities for traders to profit from short-term price movements, but it also increases the risk of

significant losses. To succeed in crypto trading, you need to be prepared for these wild swings and have a solid risk management plan in place.
- **Liquidity**: Liquidity refers to how easily an asset can be bought or sold without affecting its price. While major cryptocurrencies like Bitcoin and Ethereum tend to have high liquidity, many altcoins suffer from low liquidity, which can make it difficult to enter or exit positions at your desired price. Low liquidity can also lead to slippage—where the price moves against you as you execute your trade—so it's important to consider liquidity when choosing which cryptocurrencies to trade.
- **Security Risks**: The decentralized nature of cryptocurrencies comes with unique security risks. Unlike traditional financial systems, where transactions can be reversed or disputed, crypto transactions are irreversible once confirmed. This means that if your funds are stolen or lost (for example, through hacking or phishing), there's no way to recover them. To protect your assets, it's essential to use secure wallets, enable two-factor authentication, and be cautious of phishing scams and other security threats.
- **Market Hours**: Unlike traditional financial markets, which have set trading hours, the cryptocurrency market operates 24/7. This means that prices can change rapidly at any time of day or night, and news or events can have an immediate impact on the market. For traders, this

requires constant vigilance and the ability to react quickly to market movements.

- **Regulatory Uncertainty**: Cryptocurrency regulation varies widely by country, and the regulatory landscape is constantly evolving. While some countries have embraced cryptocurrencies and developed clear regulatory frameworks, others have imposed strict restrictions or outright bans. This regulatory uncertainty can create additional risks for traders, as changes in regulation can have a significant impact on the market.

Understanding these unique aspects of crypto trading is essential for navigating this fast-paced and often unpredictable market. By being aware of the risks and challenges, you can develop strategies to protect your capital and take advantage of the opportunities that arise.

Crypto Trading Strategies: From HODLing to Day Trading

Now that you have a solid understanding of the crypto market and its unique challenges, let's dive into some specific trading strategies you can use to profit from cryptocurrencies. Whether you're a long-term investor or a short-term trader, there's a strategy for everyone in the crypto world.

Day Trading Crypto: Capitalizing on Volatility

Day trading is a popular strategy in the cryptocurrency market due to its high volatility. Day traders buy and sell cryptocurrencies within the same day, aiming to profit from short-term price movements. Here's how to approach day trading in the crypto market:

- **Focus on Liquid Assets**: When day trading, it's important to focus on cryptocurrencies with high liquidity, such as Bitcoin, Ethereum, and other major coins. High liquidity ensures that you can enter and exit positions quickly without significant slippage.
- **Use Technical Analysis**: Technical analysis is your best friend in day trading. Use tools like moving averages, RSI, MACD, and Bollinger Bands to identify trends, overbought or oversold conditions, and potential entry and exit points. Keep an eye on key support and resistance levels, as well as volume, to confirm the strength of price movements.
- **Set Tight Stop-Losses**: Given the high volatility of the crypto market, it's crucial to set tight stop-losses to protect your capital. A tight stop-loss ensures that you exit a losing trade quickly before it turns into a larger loss.
- **Stay Informed**: The crypto market is highly sensitive to news and events, so staying informed is key. Follow crypto news sources, social media, and market analysis to stay on top of developments that could impact prices. Be prepared to act quickly if there's a major news event, such as a regulatory announcement or a significant technological development.

Day trading crypto can be highly profitable, but it's also risky and requires constant attention. If you're someone who thrives in fast-paced environments and enjoys analyzing charts, day trading might be the right strategy for you.

Swing Trading Crypto: Riding the Momentum

Swing trading is a medium-term strategy that involves holding positions for several days or weeks to capture price swings. It's less intense than day trading but still takes advantage of the crypto market's volatility. Here's how to approach swing trading in the crypto market:

- **Identify Trends**: The first step in swing trading is to identify the overall trend of the cryptocurrency you're trading. Use moving averages and trendlines to determine whether the market is in an uptrend, downtrend, or consolidation phase. Swing traders aim to enter trades in the direction of the prevailing trend.
- **Look for Reversals**: Swing traders often look for reversal patterns, such as double tops or bottoms, head and shoulders, or bullish or bearish divergences in indicators like RSI or MACD. These patterns can signal that a trend is about to reverse, offering an opportunity to enter a trade early.
- **Set Target Prices**: Before entering a trade, set a target price where you'll take profits. This target should be based on key resistance or support levels, Fibonacci retracement levels, or other

technical indicators. By setting a target price, you ensure that you lock in profits when the market reaches your desired level.
- **Be Patient**: Unlike day trading, swing trading requires patience. You'll need to wait for the right setup and be willing to hold your position for several days or weeks to capture the full price swing. Avoid the temptation to exit trades too early—let the market work in your favor.

Swing trading is ideal for traders who prefer a more measured approach and are comfortable holding positions for longer periods. It offers the potential for significant profits while allowing for more flexibility than day trading.

HODLing: Long-Term Crypto Investment

HODLing (a misspelling of "hold" that has become a popular term in the crypto community) is a long-term investment strategy that involves buying and holding cryptocurrencies for an extended period, regardless of short-term price fluctuations. Here's how to approach HODLing:

- **Choose Strong Projects**: When HODLing, it's important to invest in cryptocurrencies with strong fundamentals and long-term potential. Focus on projects with solid technology, a clear use case, and a strong development team. Bitcoin and Ethereum are popular choices for HODLing, but there are other promising projects worth considering.

- **Ignore Short-Term Volatility**: The key to successful HODLing is ignoring short-term price volatility. Cryptocurrencies are known for their wild price swings, but HODLers stay focused on the long-term potential of their investments. This means resisting the urge to sell during market downturns and maintaining confidence in your chosen assets.
- **Dollar-Cost Averaging**: One strategy that can complement HODLing is dollar-cost averaging (DCA). DCA involves investing a fixed amount of money in a cryptocurrency at regular intervals, regardless of the price. This strategy reduces the impact of market volatility and can result in a lower average purchase price over time.
- **Stay Informed**: While HODLing is a long-term strategy, it's still important to stay informed about developments in the crypto market. Keep an eye on news, technological advancements, and regulatory changes that could impact the long-term prospects of your investments.

HODLing is a great strategy for investors who believe in the long-term potential of cryptocurrencies and are willing to weather short-term market fluctuations. It's a low-maintenance approach that can yield significant returns if you choose the right assets.

Arbitrage: Exploiting Price Differences

Arbitrage is a strategy that involves taking advantage of price differences for the same cryptocurrency on different exchanges. For example, if Bitcoin is trading at $50,000 on one exchange and $50,500 on another, an arbitrage trader could buy on the cheaper exchange and sell on the more expensive one, pocketing the difference. Here's how to approach arbitrage in the crypto market:

- **Monitor Multiple Exchanges**: The first step in arbitrage is to monitor prices across multiple exchanges. This can be done manually, but many traders use arbitrage bots that automatically scan exchanges for price discrepancies.
- **Act Quickly**: Arbitrage opportunities are often short-lived, as traders quickly act to close the price gap. This means you need to act quickly to execute your trades before the opportunity disappears. Speed is critical in arbitrage trading.
- **Consider Fees and Slippage**: When calculating potential profits, be sure to consider transaction fees and the possibility of slippage (the price moving against you as you execute your trades). These factors can eat into your profits, so it's important to ensure that the price difference is large enough to cover these costs.
- **Manage Risk**: Arbitrage may seem like a low-risk strategy, but there are still risks involved. For example, there's the risk of delays in transferring funds between exchanges, which could result in missing the price difference. To manage risk, consider keeping funds on multiple exchanges to facilitate faster trades.

Arbitrage is a more advanced strategy that requires quick decision-making and careful consideration of costs. While the profit margins are typically small, the ability to execute multiple trades quickly can result in significant gains.

ICO and DeFi: Investing in the New Frontier

Initial Coin Offerings (ICOs) and Decentralized Finance (DeFi) projects represent some of the most innovative and high-risk opportunities in the crypto market. Here's how to approach these emerging areas:

- **Research ICOs Thoroughly**: ICOs are a way for new cryptocurrency projects to raise funds by selling tokens to investors. While some ICOs have resulted in significant returns, others have turned out to be scams or failures. Before investing in an ICO, research the project thoroughly. Look at the team behind the project, the technology, the whitepaper, and the roadmap. Be wary of projects that make unrealistic promises or lack transparency.
- **Understand DeFi Protocols**: DeFi is a rapidly growing area of the crypto market that aims to recreate traditional financial services—like lending, borrowing, and trading—on decentralized platforms using cryptocurrencies. DeFi protocols can offer high yields, but they also come with high risks, including smart contract vulnerabilities, market volatility, and liquidity risks. Before

investing in DeFi, make sure you understand how the protocol works and the risks involved.
- **Diversify Your Investments**: Given the high risk associated with ICOs and DeFi projects, it's important to diversify your investments. Don't put all your money into a single project or protocol. Instead, spread your investments across multiple projects to reduce your overall risk.
- **Stay Informed About Regulatory Changes**: The regulatory environment for ICOs and DeFi is still evolving, and changes in regulation could have a significant impact on these markets. Stay informed about regulatory developments in your country and consider the potential risks associated with changes in the legal landscape.

ICOs and DeFi offer the potential for high rewards, but they also come with high risks. If you're willing to take on these risks, they can be an exciting and profitable area of the crypto market to explore.

Wrapping It Up

Cryptocurrency trading is not for the faint of heart, but for those who are willing to embrace the volatility and uncertainty, it offers a wealth of opportunities. Whether you're day trading, swing trading, HODLing, or exploring new frontiers like DeFi, the key to success is to stay informed, manage your risk, and be prepared for the unexpected.

In the next chapter, we'll dive into **Advanced Trading Concepts**—covering topics like options trading, futures and commodities, forex trading, and more. This chapter will help you expand your trading toolkit and explore new markets beyond stocks and cryptocurrencies. If you're ready to take your trading to the next level, you won't want to miss it.

Until then, take some time to review your crypto trading strategies and consider how you can apply what you've learned in this chapter to your own trading journey. Remember, the crypto market is fast-moving and unpredictable, but with the right knowledge and approach, you can navigate it successfully and profitably.

Chapter 8: Advanced Trading Concepts

Stepping Up Your Game: Why Advanced Trading Concepts Matter

So, you've got a solid handle on stocks and cryptocurrencies, and you've been making some decent trades. But if you're looking to expand your toolkit and explore new markets, it's time to dive into the world of advanced trading concepts. This chapter will introduce you to trading options, futures, commodities, and forex—markets that can offer significant opportunities for those who know how to navigate them.

Trading these instruments isn't just about diversifying your portfolio; it's about understanding the unique dynamics of each market and using them to your advantage. Whether you're looking to hedge your existing positions, speculate on price movements, or leverage your capital, these advanced concepts can help you achieve your trading goals. But fair warning: with greater complexity comes greater risk, so it's crucial to understand what you're getting into before diving headfirst into these markets.

Options Trading: Flexibility and Leverage

Options trading is a versatile and powerful tool that allows you to take advantage of price movements without actually owning the underlying asset. Options can be used for a variety of purposes, including hedging, speculating, and generating income. Here's how options work and how you can use them in your trading strategy:

UNDERSTANDING THE BASICS OF OPTIONS

An option is a contract that gives the buyer the right, but not the obligation, to buy or sell an underlying asset at a specific price (the strike price) on or before a specific date (the expiration date). There are two main types of options:

- **Call Options**: A call option gives the buyer the right to buy the underlying asset at the strike price. Traders buy call options when they expect the price of the asset to rise.
- **Put Options**: A put option gives the buyer the right to sell the underlying asset at the strike price. Traders buy put options when they expect the price of the asset to fall.

Options are priced based on several factors, including the current price of the underlying asset, the strike price, the time remaining until expiration, and market volatility. The price of an option is known as the premium, and it's what the buyer pays to the seller (or writer) of the option.

STRATEGIES FOR TRADING OPTIONS

Options offer a range of strategies that can be tailored to your market outlook and risk tolerance. Here are some of the most common options trading strategies:

- **Buying Calls and Puts**: The simplest strategy is to buy call options if you expect the price of the underlying asset to rise, or put options if you expect it to fall. This strategy allows you to leverage your capital, as the cost of the option is typically much lower than the cost of buying the underlying asset outright. However, if the asset doesn't move in your favor, you could lose the entire premium paid for the option.

- **Covered Calls**: A covered call strategy involves holding a long position in an asset (such as a stock) and selling a call option on that asset. This strategy is used to generate income from the premium received from selling the option, while also providing some downside protection. If the price of the asset remains below the strike price, the option expires worthless, and you keep the premium. If the price rises above the strike price, you may have to sell the asset at the strike price, potentially missing out on further gains.
- **Protective Puts**: A protective put strategy involves buying a put option on an asset you already own. This strategy acts as an insurance policy, protecting you from a significant decline in the asset's price. If the price falls below the strike price, the put option increases in value, offsetting some or all of the losses from the decline in the underlying asset.
- **Straddles and Strangles**: These strategies involve buying both a call and a put option on the same asset with the same expiration date. A straddle involves buying options with the same strike price, while a strangle involves buying options with different strike prices. These strategies are used when you expect significant volatility in the asset's

price but are unsure of the direction. If the asset's price moves significantly in either direction, one of the options will become profitable.
- **Iron Condors**: An iron condor is a more advanced options strategy that involves selling an out-of-the-money call and put option, while simultaneously buying a further out-of-the-money call and put option. This strategy is used when you expect low volatility in the asset's price and want to generate income from the premiums received. The maximum profit is limited to the premiums received, while the maximum loss is limited to the difference between the strike prices of the options.

Options trading offers flexibility and leverage, but it also comes with significant risks. It's essential to thoroughly understand the mechanics of options and the risks involved before incorporating them into your trading strategy.

Futures Trading: Betting on the Future

Futures trading involves buying or selling contracts that obligate the trader to buy or sell an asset at a predetermined price on a specific date in the future. Futures contracts are commonly used for commodities, currencies, and financial indices, and they offer opportunities for hedging, speculation, and arbitrage. Here's how futures trading works and how you can use it to your advantage:

UNDERSTANDING THE BASICS OF FUTURES

A futures contract is an agreement between two parties to buy or sell an asset at a future date for a price agreed upon today. Unlike options, futures contracts are obligations—you are required to fulfill the contract by buying or selling the underlying asset at the agreed-upon price when the contract expires.

Futures contracts are standardized, meaning they have specific terms regarding the quantity of the underlying asset, the expiration date, and the settlement process. They are traded on futures exchanges, such as the Chicago Mercantile Exchange (CME), and are often used by producers and consumers of commodities to hedge against price fluctuations.

STRATEGIES FOR TRADING FUTURES

Futures trading offers several strategies, depending on your market outlook and risk tolerance. Here are some common futures trading strategies:

- **Directional Trading**: Directional trading involves buying or selling futures contracts based on your expectation of the future price movement of the underlying asset. For example, if you believe the price of crude oil will rise, you can buy (go long) a crude oil futures contract. If the price rises, you can sell the contract at a profit. Conversely, if you believe the price will fall, you can sell (go short) a futures contract and profit if the price declines.
- **Hedging**: Hedging is a risk management strategy used by producers and consumers of commodities to protect against adverse price movements. For

example, a farmer might sell futures contracts on corn to lock in a price for their crop, reducing the risk of a price decline before harvest. Similarly, an airline might buy futures contracts on jet fuel to lock in a price and protect against rising fuel costs.

- **Spread Trading**: Spread trading involves buying one futures contract and selling another related contract simultaneously. The goal is to profit from the price difference (spread) between the two contracts. For example, a trader might buy a December crude oil futures contract and sell a January crude oil futures contract, betting that the price difference between the two contracts will widen or narrow.
- **Calendar Spreads**: A calendar spread is a type of spread trade that involves buying and selling futures contracts with different expiration dates on the same underlying asset. The goal is to profit from changes in the price difference between the two contracts as the expiration dates approach.
- **Arbitrage**: Arbitrage involves taking advantage of price discrepancies between different markets or contracts. For example, if the price of a futures contract is different on two exchanges, a trader might buy the contract on one exchange and sell it on another, profiting from the price difference.

Futures trading offers significant leverage, as only a small percentage of the contract's value (known as margin) is required to enter a trade. However, this leverage also increases the risk, as even small price movements can result in substantial gains or losses. It's important to thoroughly understand the mechanics of futures contracts and have a solid risk management plan in place before trading futures.

Commodities Trading: Profiting from Raw Materials

Commodities trading involves buying and selling raw materials, such as gold, silver, crude oil, natural gas, and agricultural products like wheat, corn, and soybeans. Commodities are essential to the global economy, and their prices can be influenced by a wide range of factors, including supply and demand, geopolitical events, weather conditions, and economic data. Here's how commodities trading works and how you can profit from it:

UNDERSTANDING THE BASICS OF COMMODITIES TRADING

Commodities can be traded in several ways, including through futures contracts, options, and exchange-traded funds (ETFs). Futures contracts are the most common way to trade commodities, as they allow traders to speculate on the future price of the commodity without having to take physical delivery of the asset.

Commodities are typically divided into two categories:

- **Hard Commodities**: These are natural resources that are extracted or mined, such as gold, silver, crude oil, natural gas, and copper.
- **Soft Commodities**: These are agricultural products that are grown or harvested, such as wheat, corn, soybeans, coffee, sugar, and cotton.

Commodities prices can be highly volatile, making them attractive to traders who are looking to profit from price movements. However, this volatility also increases the risk, so it's important to approach commodities trading with a well-thought-out strategy and risk management plan.

STRATEGIES FOR TRADING COMMODITIES

Commodities trading offers several strategies, depending on your market outlook and risk tolerance. Here are some common commodities trading strategies:

- **Trend Following**: Trend following involves identifying and trading in the direction of the prevailing trend in the commodity's price. Traders use technical analysis tools, such as moving averages, trendlines, and the Relative Strength Index (RSI), to identify trends and enter trades in the direction of the trend. Trend following works well in commodities markets, as they often exhibit strong, sustained trends due to supply and demand imbalances.
- **Range Trading**: Range trading involves buying and selling commodities within a defined price range. Traders identify key support and resistance levels and buy at support and sell at resistance. This strategy works well in markets that are trading sideways, with no clear trend in either direction.
- **Seasonal Trading**: Seasonal trading takes advantage of predictable patterns in commodity prices that occur at certain times of the year. For

example, agricultural commodities like wheat and corn often exhibit seasonal price patterns based on planting and harvest cycles. Traders use historical price data and seasonal charts to identify these patterns and enter trades accordingly.

- **Fundamental Analysis**: Fundamental analysis involves analyzing supply and demand factors that influence the price of a commodity. For example, a trader might analyze weather patterns, crop reports, or geopolitical events that could impact the supply of a commodity like oil or wheat. By understanding the fundamental drivers of price, traders can make informed decisions about when to enter and exit trades.
- **Pairs Trading**: Pairs trading involves trading two related commodities against each other. For example, a trader might buy crude oil and sell natural gas, betting that the price of crude oil will outperform natural gas. This strategy is often used to take advantage of price discrepancies between related commodities.

Commodities trading offers the potential for significant profits, but it also comes with unique risks, including price volatility and the impact of external factors like weather and geopolitics. It's important to thoroughly understand the market dynamics of the commodities you're trading and to have a solid risk management plan in place.

Forex Trading: The World's Largest Market

Forex trading, or foreign exchange trading, involves buying and selling currencies in the global currency markets. The forex market is the largest and most liquid market in the world, with trillions of dollars traded daily. Forex trading offers opportunities for hedging, speculation, and arbitrage, and it operates 24 hours a day, five days a week. Here's how forex trading works and how you can profit from it:

UNDERSTANDING THE BASICS OF FOREX TRADING

Forex trading involves buying one currency and selling another simultaneously. Currencies are traded in pairs, such as EUR/USD (Euro/US Dollar), GBP/JPY (British Pound/Japanese Yen), or AUD/CAD (Australian Dollar/Canadian Dollar). The first currency in the pair is the base currency, and the second currency is the quote currency. The exchange rate represents how much of the quote currency you need to buy one unit of the base currency.

For example, if the EUR/USD exchange rate is 1.2000, it means that 1 Euro is worth 1.20 US Dollars. If you believe that the Euro will strengthen against the Dollar, you would buy the EUR/USD pair (go long). If the exchange rate rises to 1.2500, you can sell the pair at a profit. Conversely, if you believe the Euro will weaken against the Dollar, you would sell the EUR/USD pair (go short) and profit if the exchange rate declines.

Forex trading is typically done using leverage, which allows traders to control larger positions with a smaller amount of capital. However, leverage also increases the risk, as even small price movements can result in significant gains or losses.

STRATEGIES FOR TRADING FOREX

Forex trading offers several strategies, depending on your market outlook and risk tolerance. Here are some common forex trading strategies:

- **Scalping**: Scalping is a short-term trading strategy that involves making multiple trades throughout the day to capture small price movements. Scalpers typically hold positions for a few minutes or seconds, aiming to profit from the bid-ask spread and small price fluctuations. Scalping requires a high level of focus and quick decision-making, as well as access to real-time market data.
- **Day Trading**: Day trading in the forex market involves entering and exiting trades within the same day, typically holding positions for a few hours or minutes. Day traders use technical analysis tools, such as moving averages, RSI, and Bollinger Bands, to identify short-term trends and entry and exit points. Day trading requires a strong understanding of market dynamics and the ability to react quickly to market movements.
- **Swing Trading**: Swing trading is a medium-term strategy that involves holding positions for several days or weeks to capture price swings. Swing traders use technical analysis to identify trends, support and resistance levels, and potential

reversal points. This strategy allows traders to take advantage of larger price movements while avoiding the need for constant monitoring.

- **Position Trading**: Position trading is a long-term strategy that involves holding positions for weeks, months, or even years. Position traders focus on the overall trend of the currency pair and use fundamental analysis to identify long-term trends. This strategy requires patience and a strong understanding of macroeconomic factors that influence currency prices, such as interest rates, inflation, and geopolitical events.
- **Carry Trading**: Carry trading involves borrowing a currency with a low-interest rate and using the proceeds to buy a currency with a higher interest rate. The goal is to profit from the interest rate differential between the two currencies. Carry trades are often used in stable, low-volatility environments, but they can be risky if market conditions change.
- **News Trading**: News trading involves taking positions based on the outcome of economic events, such as central bank decisions, employment reports, or inflation data. News traders use economic calendars to track upcoming events and make quick decisions based on the market's reaction to the news. This strategy can be highly profitable, but it also comes with significant risk, as the market's reaction to news can be unpredictable.

Forex trading offers a wide range of opportunities, but it also comes with unique risks, including the impact of global economic events and the potential for large price swings due to leverage. It's important to thoroughly understand the mechanics of the forex market and to have a solid risk management plan in place before trading currencies.

Wrapping It Up

Advanced trading concepts, such as options, futures, commodities, and forex, offer a wealth of opportunities for traders looking to expand their horizons and diversify their portfolios. However, these markets also come with significant risks, and it's crucial to approach them with a thorough understanding of the instruments, strategies, and market dynamics involved.

In the next chapter, we'll explore **Building a Trading Career**—covering everything from developing your personal trading style to becoming a professional trader. We'll discuss the skills, mindset, and resources needed to build a successful and sustainable trading career, whether you're trading for yourself or working in a professional setting.

Until then, take some time to review the advanced concepts covered in this chapter and consider how they might fit into your overall trading strategy. Remember, the key to success in any market is knowledge, discipline, and a commitment to continuous learning.

Chapter 9: Building a Trading Career

The Journey from Novice to Pro: What It Takes to Build a Trading Career

Building a trading career isn't just about making money—it's about developing the discipline, mindset, and strategies that will allow you to navigate the ups and downs of the markets over the long term. Whether you're trading independently or aiming to work in a professional environment, the journey requires continuous learning, adaptation, and a deep understanding of yourself as a trader.

In this expanded chapter, we'll explore what it takes to move from being a novice trader to a seasoned professional. We'll discuss how to develop your personal trading style, set up your trading business, and maintain the discipline and focus needed to succeed. We'll also look at case studies of some of the most successful traders in history, providing real-world examples of what it takes to thrive in this challenging industry.

Developing Your Personal Trading Style

Your trading style is a reflection of who you are as a person—your risk tolerance, your decision-making process, and your ability to handle stress. Developing a personal trading style that aligns with your strengths and preferences is crucial for long-term success.

UNDERSTANDING YOUR PERSONALITY AND RISK TOLERANCE

Your personality plays a significant role in determining what kind of trader you'll be. Are you someone who thrives on quick decisions and fast-paced environments? Or do you prefer a more measured, long-term approach? Understanding your personality will help you choose a trading style that fits you.

Similarly, your risk tolerance will dictate the types of trades you're comfortable with. Some traders can handle the stress of high-risk, high-reward trades, while others prefer more conservative strategies that offer steady, if smaller, returns. Be honest with yourself about how much risk you're willing to take, and choose strategies that align with your comfort level.

EXPERIMENTING WITH DIFFERENT STRATEGIES

In the early stages of your trading career, it's a good idea to experiment with different strategies and markets to see what resonates with you. Try your hand at day trading, swing trading, and long-term investing. Explore different markets, from stocks and options to forex and cryptocurrencies. As you gain experience, you'll start to see which strategies work best for you and which markets you're most comfortable in.

DOCUMENTING YOUR TRADES AND PROGRESS

Keeping a trading journal is essential for any serious trader. Documenting your trades allows you to track your progress, identify patterns in your behavior, and learn from your mistakes. Record the details of each trade, including your reasons for entering and exiting, the outcome, and any emotions you felt during the process.

Over time, your journal will become a valuable resource for refining your trading style and improving your decision-making.

REFINING YOUR APPROACH

As you gain experience, you'll start to refine your trading style. This might involve focusing on a specific market or strategy, adjusting your risk management approach, or fine-tuning your entry and exit criteria. The key is to continuously evaluate your performance and make adjustments as needed. Remember, there's no one-size-fits-all approach to trading—what works for one trader might not work for another. The goal is to develop a style that suits your strengths and allows you to trade confidently and consistently.

Setting Up Your Trading Business

To transition from casual trading to a full-time career, you need to treat your trading like a business. This means setting up the right infrastructure, managing your finances effectively, and maintaining a high level of organization.

CREATING A DETAILED TRADING PLAN

A trading plan is your blueprint for success. It should outline your goals, strategies, risk management rules, and daily routine. Your trading plan should be detailed and specific, covering everything from the markets you'll trade to the criteria you'll use for entering and exiting trades. It's important to review and update your plan regularly as you gain experience and your goals evolve.

SETTING UP YOUR TRADING OFFICE

Your trading environment plays a crucial role in your success. Set up a dedicated trading office with all the tools and technology you need to trade effectively. This includes a reliable computer, high-speed internet connection, multiple monitors for tracking different markets, and trading software. Your office should be a quiet, distraction-free space where you can focus on the markets.

MANAGING YOUR FINANCES

Financial management is a critical aspect of running a trading business. This includes keeping track of your profits and losses, managing your capital, and paying taxes. Consider working with an accountant who specializes in trading to ensure you're meeting all your financial obligations and taking advantage of any tax benefits available to traders.

It's also important to set aside a portion of your profits for future growth. This might include reinvesting in your trading account, saving for retirement, or investing in continuing education and professional development.

STAYING ORGANIZED

Successful traders are highly organized. This means keeping detailed records of your trades, maintaining a schedule, and staying on top of market news and analysis. Use tools like calendars, spreadsheets, and trading journals to stay organized and ensure that nothing falls through the cracks.

BUILDING A NETWORK

Trading can be a solitary pursuit, but building a network of fellow traders and industry professionals can provide valuable support and insights. Join trading communities, attend conferences, and participate in online forums to connect with other traders. Networking can also open up opportunities for collaboration, mentorship, and even job opportunities if you decide to pursue a career in professional trading.

Maintaining Discipline and a Professional Mindset

Discipline is the foundation of any successful trading career. It's what keeps you on track, helps you manage risk, and ensures that you stick to your trading plan.

FOLLOWING YOUR TRADING PLAN

Your trading plan is your roadmap, and it's essential to follow it consistently. This means sticking to your entry and exit criteria, managing your risk according to your plan, and avoiding impulsive decisions. If you find yourself deviating from your plan, take a step back and reassess. Ask yourself why you're making these decisions and whether they align with your long-term goals.

MANAGING YOUR EMOTIONS

Emotions can be one of the biggest obstacles to success in trading. Fear, greed, overconfidence, and frustration can all lead to poor decisions and costly mistakes. Developing emotional resilience is key to maintaining discipline and staying focused on your trading goals. Techniques like mindfulness, meditation, and regular breaks can help you manage stress and maintain a clear, calm mindset.

CONTINUAL LEARNING AND IMPROVEMENT

The markets are constantly evolving, and staying competitive requires a commitment to continual learning. Invest in your education by reading books, taking courses, and attending workshops. Stay informed about market developments, new technologies, and changes in regulations. The more you learn, the better equipped you'll be to adapt to changing market conditions and seize new opportunities.

SETTING REALISTIC GOALS

Setting realistic, achievable goals is essential for staying motivated and maintaining discipline. Break your long-term goals down into smaller, actionable steps, and track your progress regularly. Celebrate your successes, but also be prepared to adjust your goals as needed. Remember, trading is a marathon, not a sprint, and it's important to focus on consistent progress over time.

Transitioning to Professional Trading

If you're interested in taking your trading career to the next level, you might consider becoming a professional trader. Professional traders work for financial institutions, hedge funds, or proprietary trading firms, and they often have access to more capital, resources, and opportunities than independent traders. Here's how to pursue a career as a professional trader:

GAINING EXPERIENCE AND BUILDING A TRACK RECORD

Before you can land a job as a professional trader, you'll need to gain experience and build a track record of success. This means consistently profitable trading over an extended period and maintaining detailed records of your trades. Your track record is your most valuable asset when applying for trading positions, so make sure it's well-documented and reflects your skills and abilities.

PURSUING EDUCATION AND CERTIFICATIONS

Many professional trading positions require a strong educational background, often in fields like finance, economics, or mathematics. Additionally, certifications like the Chartered Financial Analyst (CFA) or Financial Risk Manager (FRM) can enhance your credentials and make you more competitive in the job market.

NETWORKING AND BUILDING CONNECTIONS

As with any career, networking is key to landing a job as a professional trader. Attend industry events, join professional organizations, and connect with traders and recruiters on LinkedIn. Building relationships with industry professionals can open doors to job opportunities and provide valuable insights into the trading world.

APPLYING TO TRADING FIRMS

Once you've gained experience and built a strong track record, you can start applying to trading firms. Look for positions at hedge funds, investment banks, proprietary trading firms, and asset management companies. Be prepared for a rigorous interview process, which may include technical assessments, trading simulations, and behavioral interviews.

CONTINUING TO DEVELOP YOUR SKILLS

Even after landing a professional trading job, it's important to continue developing your skills and knowledge. The financial industry is constantly changing, and staying competitive requires ongoing learning and adaptation. Take advantage of any training and development opportunities offered by your employer, and stay proactive in seeking out new knowledge and experiences.

Case Studies of Successful Traders

Real-world examples of successful traders provide valuable insights into what it takes to build a thriving trading career. Here are case studies of four legendary traders, each with unique approaches and lessons to offer.

CASE STUDY 1: PAUL TUDOR JONES

- **Background and Early Career**: Paul Tudor Jones is one of the most successful and well-known traders in the world. He started his career as a commodities broker before founding Tudor Investment Corporation, a hedge fund that has consistently delivered strong returns.
- **Key Trades and Strategies**: Jones is best known for his ability to predict and profit from the 1987 stock market crash, where he reportedly tripled

his money using short positions. His trading style is heavily focused on macroeconomic analysis and technical indicators.

- **Lessons from His Approach**: Jones emphasizes the importance of risk management and capital preservation. He is known for saying, "The most important rule of trading is to play great defense, not great offense." His disciplined approach to risk has been a key factor in his long-term success.

CASE STUDY 2: LINDA RASCHKE

- **Transition from Independent to Professional Trading**: Linda Raschke began her trading career on the floor of the Pacific Coast Stock Exchange before transitioning to independent trading. She later managed money for clients and became a well-respected figure in the trading community.
- **Notable Strategies and Discipline**: Raschke is known for her disciplined approach to trading and her focus on developing routines. She employs a variety of strategies, including swing trading and pattern recognition, and is a strong advocate for keeping a trading journal.
- **Insights into Her Mindset**: Raschke emphasizes the importance of routine and discipline in trading. She believes that consistent execution of a well-thought-out plan is more important than trying to predict market movements. Her success is a testament to the power of disciplined trading.

CASE STUDY 3: STANLEY DRUCKENMILLER

- **Macro Trading and Risk Management**: Stanley Druckenmiller is a legendary macro trader who worked alongside George Soros at the Quantum Fund. He is known for his ability to manage large amounts of capital and for his skill in making big bets on macroeconomic trends.
- **Key Trades**: Druckenmiller's most famous trade was his involvement in shorting the British pound in 1992, which became known as "Black Wednesday." This trade reportedly earned the Quantum Fund over $1 billion.
- **Lessons on Risk and Reward**: Druckenmiller has said that he focuses on maximizing returns while minimizing risk, often by making a few large, well-researched bets rather than spreading his capital across many smaller positions. His approach underscores the importance of conviction in trading.

CASE STUDY 4: WILLIAM O'NEIL

- **The CANSLIM Strategy**: William O'Neil is the founder of Investor's Business Daily and the creator of the CANSLIM strategy, a method for identifying high-growth stocks based on specific criteria. His approach combines technical and fundamental analysis to find winning stocks.
- **Research and Innovation**: O'Neil's success is rooted in his dedication to research and innovation. He spent years studying the best-performing stocks in history to develop the

CANSLIM method, which has been widely adopted by growth investors.
- **Combining Analysis Techniques**: O'Neil's strategy highlights the power of combining technical and fundamental analysis to find stocks with strong growth potential. His work is a reminder of the importance of continuous research and adaptation in trading.

Final Thoughts on Building a Sustainable Trading Career

Building a trading career is a marathon, not a sprint. The key to long-term success lies in developing a trading style that aligns with your strengths, managing your trading business with professionalism and discipline, and continually learning and adapting to the markets.

As you move forward in your trading journey, remember that the most successful traders are those who maintain a balance between confidence and humility, who are always willing to learn and adapt, and who never lose sight of the importance of risk management. Whether you choose to trade independently or pursue a career in professional trading, focus on building a sustainable approach that can weather the inevitable ups and downs of the markets.

Chapter 10: Trading Technology and Tools

The Evolution of Trading Technology

Trading has come a long way from the days of ticker tapes and crowded trading floors. The evolution of trading technology has not only democratized access to markets but has also transformed the way traders analyze, execute, and manage their trades. Understanding this evolution is crucial for modern traders who want to leverage the latest tools and technologies to gain an edge in the markets.

Historical Overview of Trading Tools

In the early 20th century, traders relied on ticker tapes to get real-time price information. The "ticker tape" was a thin strip of paper that printed stock symbols and prices in almost real-time, giving traders the data they needed to make decisions. This system, while groundbreaking at the time, was slow and prone to errors, with traders needing to manually track prices and calculate positions.

The 1970s and 1980s saw the introduction of electronic trading platforms, which revolutionized the industry. With the advent of computers and electronic exchanges, traders could now access real-time price information, execute trades more quickly, and manage their portfolios more efficiently. The introduction of personal computers and the internet in the 1990s further accelerated this trend, making trading accessible to anyone with a computer and an internet connection.

Today, trading is a high-tech endeavor, with sophisticated platforms, algorithms, and tools that can analyze massive amounts of data, execute trades in microseconds, and manage risk with precision. This evolution has opened up new opportunities for traders, but it has also made the markets more competitive and complex.

Essential Tools for Modern Traders

To be successful in today's fast-paced markets, traders need to equip themselves with the right tools. These tools not only help you analyze the markets but also enable you to execute your strategies more effectively and manage your risk more efficiently.

Trading Platforms and Software

The trading platform is the cornerstone of your trading setup. It's where you execute trades, analyze markets, and manage your portfolio. Here are some key features to look for in a trading platform:

- **User Interface**: A clean, intuitive interface makes it easier to execute trades quickly and efficiently.
- **Order Types**: The platform should support various order types (market, limit, stop-loss, etc.) to give you flexibility in executing your trades.
- **Charting Tools**: Robust charting tools are essential for technical analysis. Look for platforms that offer a wide range of indicators, drawing tools, and customizable charts.
- **Data Feeds**: Real-time data feeds are crucial for making informed trading decisions. Ensure your

platform provides accurate and timely market data.
- **Execution Speed**: In fast-moving markets, execution speed can be the difference between a profit and a loss. Choose a platform known for its reliability and speed.

Charting Tools and Technical Analysis Software

Technical analysis is a vital part of trading, and having the right charting tools can significantly enhance your ability to identify trends, patterns, and key levels in the market.

- **Chart Types**: Look for software that offers a variety of chart types (candlestick, bar, line, etc.) to suit different analysis styles.
- **Indicators and Overlays**: Essential indicators like moving averages, RSI, MACD, Bollinger Bands, and Fibonacci retracement should be available. The ability to overlay multiple indicators is also important.
- **Customizability**: The best charting tools allow you to customize the look and feel of your charts, create custom indicators, and save chart templates for future use.
- **Backtesting Capabilities**: Some advanced charting tools offer backtesting features, allowing you to test your strategies against historical data before applying them in live markets.

News Aggregators and Market Scanners

Staying informed is crucial in trading, and having access to real-time news and market data can give you an edge. News aggregators and market scanners help you keep track of important developments that can affect your trades.

- **News Aggregators**: These tools pull in news from various sources and provide real-time updates on market-moving events. Some popular options include Bloomberg, Reuters, and financial news sections on trading platforms.
- **Market Scanners**: Market scanners allow you to filter and search for specific stocks, forex pairs, or commodities based on criteria like price, volume, volatility, or technical indicators. These tools can help you identify potential trading opportunities quickly.

Algorithmic and Automated Trading

As technology has advanced, so too has the sophistication of trading strategies. Algorithmic and automated trading systems have become increasingly popular, allowing traders to execute complex strategies with precision and efficiency.

Introduction to Algorithmic Trading

Algorithmic trading, or algo trading, involves using computer programs to execute trades based on predefined criteria. These algorithms can process vast amounts of data, identify trading opportunities, and execute trades at speeds impossible for humans.

- **How It Works**: Algorithms are typically based on mathematical models and statistical analysis. Traders program these algorithms to follow specific rules, such as buying a stock when it drops below a certain price or selling when a particular indicator crosses a threshold.
- **Types of Algorithms**: Common types of trading algorithms include trend-following algorithms, mean-reversion algorithms, and arbitrage algorithms. Each type of algorithm is designed to exploit different market conditions.

Building and Backtesting Trading Algorithms

Before deploying an algorithm in live markets, it's essential to test it thoroughly. This process, known as backtesting, involves running the algorithm against historical market data to see how it would have performed.

- **Backtesting Platforms**: Many trading platforms offer built-in backtesting tools that allow you to test your algorithms using historical data. You can also use dedicated software like MetaTrader or NinjaTrader for more advanced backtesting.
- **Key Metrics**: When backtesting, look at metrics like profit factor, maximum drawdown, win/loss ratio, and Sharpe ratio to assess the performance of your algorithm.
- **Optimization**: Once you've backtested your algorithm, you may need to tweak its parameters to optimize performance. However, be cautious of

overfitting, which occurs when an algorithm is too finely tuned to historical data and may not perform well in live markets.

Pros and Cons of Automated Trading Systems

Automated trading systems offer several advantages, but they also come with risks.

- **Pros**:
    - **Speed**: Automated systems can execute trades much faster than humans, taking advantage of market opportunities that might otherwise be missed.
    - **Discipline**: Automated trading removes the emotional component, ensuring that trades are executed according to the predefined strategy.
    - **Efficiency**: Algorithms can monitor multiple markets and securities simultaneously, something that would be impossible for a human trader.
- **Cons**:
    - **Technical Risks**: Automated systems are prone to technical failures, such as software bugs or connectivity issues, which can lead to unexpected losses.
    - **Over-Optimization**: As mentioned, over-optimizing an algorithm can result in poor performance in live markets, as the algorithm may be too tailored to past data.

- **Lack of Flexibility**: Automated systems follow strict rules, which can be a disadvantage in rapidly changing market conditions where human judgment might be more effective.

Leveraging Artificial Intelligence and Machine Learning

Artificial intelligence (AI) and machine learning (ML) are at the forefront of trading technology, offering new ways to analyze data, identify patterns, and predict market movements.

The Role of AI and Machine Learning in Modern Trading

AI and ML have the potential to revolutionize trading by processing and analyzing massive amounts of data more efficiently than traditional methods. These technologies can identify patterns and trends that are not immediately apparent to human traders.

- **Predictive Analytics**: AI algorithms can analyze historical data to predict future price movements, giving traders a potential edge in the markets.
- **Natural Language Processing**: Some AI systems use natural language processing (NLP) to analyze news articles, social media posts, and other text-based data sources to gauge market sentiment and predict price changes.
- **Reinforcement Learning**: This advanced form of machine learning involves algorithms that learn

from their trading experiences, improving their performance over time by continuously refining their strategies based on past outcomes.

How Traders Are Using AI to Predict Market Movements

- **Sentiment Analysis**: Traders use AI to analyze social media sentiment and news reports to predict how market participants might react to certain events.
- **Price Forecasting**: Machine learning models can be trained on historical price data to forecast future price movements with varying degrees of accuracy.
- **Risk Management**: AI systems can automatically adjust trading strategies in real-time based on changing market conditions, helping traders manage risk more effectively.

Ethical Considerations and Potential Risks

While AI and machine learning offer significant advantages, they also raise ethical concerns and potential risks.

- **Market Manipulation**: There is concern that sophisticated AI algorithms could be used to manipulate markets, particularly in less liquid assets.
- **Transparency**: AI systems often operate as "black boxes," meaning their decision-making processes are not fully transparent. This lack of transparency

can make it difficult to understand why certain trades were made.
- **Bias in Algorithms**: AI systems are only as good as the data they are trained on. If the data contains biases, the algorithm's decisions will reflect those biases, potentially leading to unintended and unfair outcomes.

Risk Management Tools

Effective risk management is crucial for long-term success in trading. Fortunately, there are a variety of tools available to help you manage risk more effectively.

Stop-Loss and Take-Profit Automation

Automating your stop-loss and take-profit orders is one of the simplest yet most effective ways to manage risk.

- **Stop-Loss Orders**: These orders automatically sell a position when it reaches a certain price, limiting your losses if the market moves against you.
- **Take-Profit Orders**: These orders automatically close a position when it reaches a predetermined profit level, ensuring you lock in gains before the market reverses.
- **Trailing Stops**: A trailing stop is a dynamic stop-loss order that moves with the market price, allowing you to lock in profits while giving the position room to run.

Portfolio Management Software and Risk Analytics

Managing a portfolio of assets requires sophisticated tools that can help you monitor risk and optimize your asset allocation.

- **Risk Analytics**: Tools like Value at Risk (VaR), stress testing, and scenario analysis can help you assess the potential impact of adverse market movements on your portfolio.
- **Portfolio Management Software**: Software like Portfolio123 and Morningstar Direct allows you to track your portfolio's performance, rebalance your holdings, and analyze your risk exposure.

Stress Testing Your Trading Strategies

Stress testing involves running simulations to see how your trading strategies would perform under different market conditions.

- **Scenario Analysis**: This involves testing your strategies against historical market events, such as the 2008 financial crisis, to see how they would have held up.
- **Monte Carlo Simulations**: These simulations use random sampling to model thousands of potential market scenarios, giving you a sense of how your strategies might perform in the future.

Emerging Technologies: Blockchain and Decentralized Finance (DeFi)

Blockchain technology and decentralized finance (DeFi) are two of the most exciting developments in the world of trading. These technologies are opening up new opportunities and challenges for traders.

The Impact of Blockchain on Trading and Finance

Blockchain technology, which underpins cryptocurrencies like Bitcoin and Ethereum, is a decentralized ledger that records transactions across a network of computers. This technology has the potential to revolutionize the trading industry.

- **Transparency**: Blockchain provides a transparent and immutable record of transactions, reducing the risk of fraud and increasing trust among market participants.
- **Efficiency**: Blockchain can streamline the settlement process, reducing the time and cost of trading securities.
- **Tokenization**: Blockchain allows for the tokenization of assets, enabling new forms of trading and investment, such as fractional ownership of real estate or fine art.

Trading on Decentralized Exchanges (DEXs)

Decentralized exchanges (DEXs) are platforms that allow users to trade cryptocurrencies directly with each other, without the need for a central authority.

- **How DEXs Work**: DEXs use smart contracts to facilitate trades, ensuring that transactions are secure and transparent.

- **Advantages of DEXs**: These platforms offer greater privacy, lower fees, and reduced counterparty risk compared to traditional exchanges.
- **Challenges of DEXs**: DEXs can be more complex to use, and they often have lower liquidity than centralized exchanges, which can lead to higher slippage and wider spreads.

How DeFi Is Changing the Landscape for Traders

Decentralized finance (DeFi) is a rapidly growing sector that aims to recreate traditional financial services—such as lending, borrowing, and trading—on decentralized platforms using blockchain technology.

- **DeFi Protocols**: DeFi platforms like Uniswap, Aave, and Compound allow users to trade, lend, and borrow cryptocurrencies without intermediaries.
- **Yield Farming and Staking**: DeFi also offers new opportunities for earning passive income through activities like yield farming and staking, where users provide liquidity to DeFi platforms in exchange for rewards.
- **Risks and Considerations**: While DeFi offers exciting opportunities, it also comes with significant risks, including smart contract vulnerabilities, regulatory uncertainty, and the potential for market manipulation.

Integrating Technology into Your Trading Strategy

Technology can be a powerful tool in your trading arsenal, but it's important to use it wisely. Here are some best practices for integrating technology into your trading strategy.

Best Practices for Using Technology Without Becoming Over-Reliant

- **Maintain Human Judgment**: While technology can enhance your trading, it should not replace your own judgment and analysis. Use tools to support your decisions, not to make them for you.
- **Regularly Review Your Tools**: Technology evolves quickly, so it's important to regularly review the tools and platforms you use to ensure they are still the best fit for your needs.
- **Avoid Over-Optimization**: Be cautious of over-optimizing your algorithms or trading strategies, as this can lead to poor performance in live markets.

Staying Updated with Technological Advancements

The world of trading technology is constantly evolving, and staying updated is crucial for maintaining a competitive edge.

- **Industry News**: Follow industry news sources, blogs, and forums to stay informed about the latest developments in trading technology.
- **Continuous Learning**: Take courses or attend webinars on new trading technologies to deepen your understanding and skills.

- **Experimentation**: Don't be afraid to experiment with new tools and technologies, but always test them thoroughly before incorporating them into your live trading.

Balancing Technology with Human Judgment

While technology can greatly enhance your trading, it's important to remember that it's only a tool. The most successful traders are those who can combine the power of technology with their own experience, intuition, and judgment.

- **Trust Your Instincts**: If something doesn't feel right, don't hesitate to override your technology. Trust your instincts and experience as a trader.
- **Keep Learning**: Continuously improve your understanding of the markets and trading strategies. The more knowledgeable you are, the better you'll be able to use technology effectively.
- **Adapt and Evolve**: The markets are constantly changing, and so should your approach. Stay flexible and be willing to adapt your strategies as new technologies emerge and market conditions evolve.

Wrapping It Up

Trading technology has come a long way, and today's traders have access to tools and resources that were unimaginable just a few decades ago. By understanding and leveraging these technologies, you can gain a significant edge in the markets. However, it's important to remember that technology is only one part of the equation. Successful trading requires a balance of cutting-edge tools, sound strategy, disciplined execution, and continuous learning.

In the next chapter, we'll explore **The Psychology of Successful Trading Communities**. We'll dive into the role of community in trading success, how to find or build a trading community, and how to avoid the pitfalls of groupthink. Whether you're trading alone or as part of a group, understanding the psychology of trading communities can provide valuable insights and support.

Chapter 11: The Psychology of Successful Trading Communities

The Power of Trading Communities

Trading can be a solitary endeavor, but it doesn't have to be. Being part of a trading community can provide significant psychological and practical benefits. Whether online or offline, trading communities offer a platform for sharing ideas, learning from others, and gaining support during tough times.

Why Community Matters in Trading

Trading is challenging, and it's easy to feel isolated, especially during periods of loss or uncertainty. Being part of a community can help you stay motivated, offer different perspectives, and provide a support system that keeps you grounded.

- **Emotional Support**: Trading can be an emotional rollercoaster. A community can provide emotional support, helping you stay calm and focused during difficult times.
- **Knowledge Sharing**: Communities are a great source of knowledge. By sharing strategies, insights, and experiences, members can learn from each other and improve their trading skills.
- **Accountability**: Being part of a group can create a sense of accountability. When others are aware of your goals and progress, you may feel more motivated to stick to your trading plan and stay disciplined.

Types of Trading Communities

Trading communities come in many forms, each with its own benefits and drawbacks. Finding the right community for you is essential to maximizing the benefits.

Online Forums and Social Media Groups

Online forums and social media groups are popular platforms for traders to connect, share ideas, and discuss market developments.

- **Advantages**:
    - **Accessibility**: These communities are easy to join and often have a wide range of participants, from beginners to experts.

- **Diverse Perspectives**: With participants from around the world, you'll gain insights into different markets and strategies.
- **Anonymity**: Some traders prefer the anonymity offered by online communities, which allows them to ask questions and share ideas without fear of judgment.

- **Disadvantages**:
  - **Quality of Information**: Not all information shared in these communities is accurate or reliable. It's important to vet the sources and do your own research.
  - **Groupthink**: Online communities can sometimes fall into groupthink, where the majority opinion is accepted without critical analysis.

Professional Networks and Mentorship Programs

Professional networks and mentorship programs offer a more structured and formal approach to trading communities.

- **Advantages**:
  - **Expert Guidance**: Mentorship programs connect you with experienced traders who can offer personalized advice and support.
  - **Networking Opportunities**: Professional networks provide opportunities to connect with industry professionals,

potentially leading to job offers, partnerships, or other opportunities.
  - **Focused Learning**: These communities often have a specific focus, whether it's a particular market, strategy, or trading philosophy, which can help you deepen your expertise.
- **Disadvantages**:
  - **Cost**: Many professional networks and mentorship programs charge fees, which can be a barrier for some traders.
  - **Exclusive Membership**: Some of these communities are exclusive and may require you to meet certain criteria to join.

Local Trading Clubs and Meetups

Local trading clubs and meetups offer an in-person alternative to online communities, allowing traders to connect face-to-face.

- **Advantages**:
  - **Personal Connection**: Meeting in person allows for deeper connections and more meaningful discussions.
  - **Regular Interaction**: Many local clubs meet regularly, providing consistent opportunities to learn and connect.
  - **Diverse Learning Opportunities**: Local meetups often feature guest speakers, workshops, and other learning

opportunities that can enhance your trading skills.

- **Disadvantages**:
  - **Geographical Limitations**: Local clubs are limited to traders in your area, which may result in less diversity in perspectives and experiences.
  - **Inconsistent Quality**: The quality of local clubs can vary, depending on the knowledge and experience of the members and organizers.

Finding the Right Trading Community

Not all trading communities are created equal, and finding the right one can significantly impact your trading journey. Here's how to identify a community that aligns with your goals and values.

How to Identify a Community That Aligns with Your Goals and Values

- **Define Your Goals**: Before joining a community, define what you hope to gain from it. Are you looking for education, support, networking, or something else? Understanding your goals will help you choose the right community.
- **Research the Community**: Look into the community's history, leadership, and reputation. Read reviews, ask for recommendations, and, if possible, attend a meeting or participate in a trial period before committing.

- **Evaluate the Level of Engagement**: A good trading community should have active and engaged members who contribute regularly. Look for communities where members are genuinely interested in helping each other succeed.

The Importance of Diversity in Trading Opinions and Strategies

Diversity is crucial in a trading community. Engaging with traders who have different opinions, strategies, and backgrounds can help you see the markets from multiple perspectives and challenge your own assumptions.

- **Avoiding Echo Chambers**: Communities where everyone shares the same views can become echo chambers, where critical thinking is stifled. Seek out communities that encourage debate and discussion, even if it means encountering ideas that challenge your own.
- **Learning from Different Strategies**: Engaging with traders who use different strategies can broaden your understanding of the markets and introduce you to new approaches that you might not have considered.

Evaluating the Quality of Advice and Discussions

Not all advice is good advice, and it's important to critically evaluate the information you receive in trading communities.

- **Check Credentials**: When someone offers advice, consider their background and experience. Are they a seasoned trader with a proven track record, or a novice who may not have the expertise to offer reliable advice?
- **Cross-Check Information**: Before acting on advice or information, cross-check it with other sources. This could include doing your own research, consulting other members, or seeking advice from more experienced traders.
- **Consider the Source**: Be cautious of advice from anonymous sources, particularly in online communities. While anonymity can encourage openness, it can also lead to misinformation and unverified claims.

Learning and Growing Through Community

One of the biggest benefits of being part of a trading community is the opportunity to learn and grow through collaboration and shared experiences.

Sharing Strategies and Learning from Others' Experiences

- **Strategy Sharing**: Communities provide a platform for traders to share their strategies and receive feedback. By discussing your approach with others, you can identify potential weaknesses and refine your methods.
- **Learning from Mistakes**: Hearing about others' mistakes can be just as valuable as learning from your own. Community members often share their

experiences with trades that didn't go as planned, offering valuable lessons on what to avoid.

Participating in Collaborative Trading Challenges and Competitions

- **Friendly Competition**: Many communities organize trading challenges or competitions, which can be a fun way to test your skills and learn from others. These events often simulate real trading conditions, providing a valuable learning experience.
- **Team Trading**: Some communities offer team trading exercises, where members collaborate on trades and strategies. This can help you see how others approach the markets and develop new skills.

How to Give and Receive Constructive Feedback

Constructive feedback is essential for growth, and trading communities provide a platform for both giving and receiving it.

- **Be Open to Feedback**: When sharing your trades or strategies, be open to receiving feedback from others. Even if it's critical, constructive feedback can help you identify areas for improvement.
- **Provide Thoughtful Feedback**: When giving feedback, focus on being constructive and supportive. Point out strengths as well as areas for

improvement, and offer specific suggestions on how the person can improve.
- **Avoid Negativity**: Trading is challenging, and negative or harsh feedback can be discouraging. Aim to create a positive environment where members feel comfortable sharing their experiences and learning from each other.

Avoiding the Pitfalls of Groupthink

While trading communities offer many benefits, they can also present risks, particularly when it comes to groupthink. Groupthink occurs when members of a group prioritize consensus over critical thinking, leading to poor decision-making.

Understanding the Risks of Herd Behavior in Trading

- **Herd Behavior**: In trading, herd behavior occurs when traders follow the crowd without independent analysis. This can lead to bubbles, market panics, and poor decision-making.
- **False Confidence**: Being part of a group can sometimes give traders a false sense of confidence, leading them to take on more risk than they would if trading alone.

Maintaining Your Individual Strategy While Benefiting from Group Insights

- **Stay True to Your Plan**: While it's valuable to consider the opinions and strategies of others, it's important to stay true to your trading plan. Use

the insights from the community to inform your decisions, but don't abandon your strategy in favor of the group's consensus.
- **Critical Thinking**: Always apply critical thinking to the information you receive from the community. Question assumptions, analyze the data, and make decisions based on your own research and analysis.
- **Diversify Your Sources**: Don't rely solely on one community or source of information. Engage with multiple communities, read widely, and consult a variety of experts to ensure you're getting a well-rounded view of the markets.

Building Your Own Trading Community

If you can't find a community that meets your needs, or if you have a specific vision for a trading group, consider building your own.

Steps to Start Your Own Trading Group or Forum

- **Define Your Purpose**: Start by defining the purpose of your community. What are your goals? What type of traders do you want to attract? What kind of culture do you want to create?
- **Choose a Platform**: Decide whether your community will be online or offline. Online platforms like Discord, Slack, or specialized trading forums offer flexibility and accessibility, while offline meetups provide personal connection.

- **Set Ground Rules**: Establish clear rules and guidelines for behavior, participation, and content. This will help create a positive and respectful environment where members feel safe to share and learn.
- **Promote Your Community**: To attract members, promote your community on social media, trading forums, and at industry events. Consider hosting free webinars, workshops, or Q&A sessions to generate interest.
- **Encourage Participation**: Foster an active and engaged community by encouraging members to share their experiences, ask questions, and contribute to discussions.

Creating a Positive and Productive Environment

- **Lead by Example**: As the community leader, set the tone by being respectful, supportive, and open-minded. Your behavior will influence the culture of the group.
- **Moderate Effectively**: Appoint moderators to help maintain order and enforce the community's rules. Address conflicts quickly and fairly to prevent issues from escalating.
- **Celebrate Successes**: Recognize and celebrate the achievements of community members. This can boost morale and encourage others to stay engaged and motivated.

Encouraging Diversity of Thought and Respectful Discourse

- **Welcome Different Perspectives**: Encourage members to share diverse opinions and strategies, even if they differ from the majority. This can lead to richer discussions and deeper learning.
- **Promote Respectful Debate**: Foster a culture of respectful debate, where members feel comfortable challenging ideas without fear of personal attacks. This will help prevent groupthink and promote critical thinking.
- **Focus on Learning**: Remind members that the goal of the community is learning and growth, not proving who is right or wrong. Encourage a collaborative approach where everyone contributes to each other's success.

The Future of Trading Communities

The landscape of trading communities is evolving rapidly, driven by advances in technology and changes in how traders connect and collaborate.

The Impact of Technology on Trading Communities

- **Virtual Reality and the Metaverse**: Emerging technologies like virtual reality (VR) and the metaverse could transform how traders connect and collaborate. Imagine attending virtual trading meetups, conferences, or even trading floors where you can interact with others in a fully immersive environment.
- **AI-Powered Communities**: AI could play a role in curating content, connecting members with

similar interests, or even providing personalized learning and trading recommendations within communities.
- **Decentralized Communities**: With the rise of blockchain and decentralized finance (DeFi), we may see the emergence of decentralized trading communities where members govern and manage the group collectively, without a central authority.

How Global Connectivity Is Shaping the Future of Trading Networks

- **Global Participation**: As internet access continues to expand globally, we're likely to see even greater diversity in trading communities, with participants from different cultures, markets, and backgrounds contributing unique perspectives.
- **24/7 Collaboration**: The global nature of trading means that markets are always open somewhere. Online communities enable traders to collaborate and support each other around the clock, regardless of time zones.
- **Localized Insights**: Global communities can provide localized insights into different markets, helping traders gain a deeper understanding of global economic trends and opportunities.

Wrapping It Up

Trading communities play a crucial role in the success and development of traders. Whether you're seeking emotional support, knowledge sharing, or simply a sense of belonging, being part of a trading community can significantly enhance your trading experience. However, it's important to approach communities with a critical mindset, balancing the benefits of group insights with your individual judgment and strategy.

As trading continues to evolve, so too will the communities that support it. By staying engaged, open-minded, and committed to continuous learning, you can leverage the power of trading communities to achieve your goals and thrive in the markets.

In the next and final chapter, we'll conclude the book with a **Recap of Key Concepts** and offer some final thoughts and advice on your trading journey. We'll revisit the most important lessons from the book and provide guidance on how to continue growing and thriving as a trader.

Conclusion: Recap and Final Thoughts

As we bring this book to a close, it's time to reflect on the journey we've taken together—from understanding the basics of trading to exploring advanced strategies, tools, and the psychology behind successful trading. Whether you're just starting out or looking to refine your approach, the concepts and strategies covered in this book are designed to equip you with the knowledge and mindset needed to thrive in the markets.

Recap of Key Concepts

The Foundations of Trading

We began by laying the groundwork for successful trading, covering the importance of understanding market mechanics, risk management, and the psychology of trading. These foundational elements are crucial for anyone looking to succeed in the financial markets. Without a solid grasp of these basics, even the most sophisticated strategies can falter.

- **Understanding Markets**: Knowing how different markets operate—whether stocks, forex, commodities, or cryptocurrencies—is the first step to developing a trading strategy that suits your goals and risk tolerance.
- **Risk Management**: Effective risk management is what separates successful traders from those who struggle. Whether it's position sizing, stop-loss orders, or diversification, managing your risk is key to long-term success.

- **Trading Psychology**: Emotions play a significant role in trading. Fear, greed, and overconfidence can all lead to poor decision-making. Developing mental discipline and emotional resilience is as important as any technical skill.

Building and Refining Your Trading Strategy

As you progressed through the book, we delved into various trading strategies, from technical analysis and chart patterns to more complex approaches like algorithmic trading and options. The goal was to provide you with a toolkit of strategies that you can adapt and refine based on your personal trading style and market conditions.

- **Technical Analysis**: Using tools like moving averages, RSI, and candlestick patterns can help you identify trends and make informed decisions. Technical analysis is a powerful tool when used correctly.
- **Fundamental Analysis**: Understanding the underlying factors that drive market movements, such as economic data, company earnings, and geopolitical events, is crucial for making informed long-term investments.
- **Advanced Strategies**: From options trading to algorithmic trading, we explored more sophisticated strategies that can enhance your trading performance. These require a higher level of understanding and risk tolerance but can offer significant rewards.

Leveraging Technology and Communities

In the latter chapters, we explored how modern technology and trading communities can enhance your trading experience. These elements are increasingly important in today's fast-paced, interconnected markets.

- **Trading Technology**: The right tools and platforms can give you a significant edge. Whether it's a robust trading platform, charting software, or algorithmic trading systems, technology can help you analyze markets more effectively and execute trades with precision.
- **Trading Communities**: Being part of a trading community can provide support, shared knowledge, and motivation. However, it's important to maintain your individuality and avoid the pitfalls of groupthink.

Building a Sustainable Trading Career

Finally, we focused on what it takes to build a successful and sustainable trading career. Trading is not just about making quick profits—it's about developing a long-term approach that can withstand market volatility and changes in personal circumstances.

- **Developing Your Personal Trading Style**: Finding a trading style that suits your personality and risk tolerance is key to long-term success. Experiment with different strategies, document your progress, and refine your approach over time.

- **Setting Up Your Trading Business**: Treating trading like a business means being disciplined, organized, and professional in your approach. This includes managing your finances, maintaining records, and continuously improving your skills.
- **Transitioning to Professional Trading**: If you're looking to take your trading to the next level, consider the steps needed to transition to professional trading. This includes building a track record, pursuing education and certifications, and networking within the industry.

Final Thoughts and Advice

As you continue your trading journey, remember that success in the markets is a marathon, not a sprint. It's easy to get caught up in the excitement of trading, but maintaining a long-term perspective is essential.

- **Stay Disciplined**: Discipline is the cornerstone of successful trading. Stick to your plan, manage your risk, and avoid impulsive decisions. Remember that every trade is part of a larger strategy, and consistency is key to achieving your goals.
- **Keep Learning**: The markets are always evolving, and staying informed is crucial. Whether it's new technologies, market trends, or regulatory changes, continuous learning will help you stay ahead of the curve.
- **Embrace Adaptability**: No strategy works forever. The best traders are those who can adapt to

changing market conditions, learn from their mistakes, and continuously refine their approach.
- **Balance Confidence with Humility**: Confidence is important in trading, but overconfidence can lead to risky behavior. Balance your confidence with a healthy dose of humility, recognizing that the markets are unpredictable and that there is always more to learn.

The Road Ahead

Trading offers endless opportunities, but it's also a challenging and demanding endeavor. By applying the principles and strategies discussed in this book, you're equipping yourself with the tools needed to navigate the markets successfully. However, remember that trading is a personal journey, and your success will be defined by your ability to remain disciplined, adaptable, and committed to continuous improvement.

As you move forward, take the time to reflect on your progress, celebrate your successes, and learn from your setbacks. The road to becoming a successful trader is filled with challenges, but with the right mindset and approach, it's a journey that can be both rewarding and fulfilling.

Thank you for allowing me to be part of your trading journey. I wish you success in all your future trades, and I hope this book has provided you with valuable insights and inspiration to achieve your trading goals. Remember, the markets are always open, and every day brings new opportunities—so keep learning, keep trading, and never stop striving for success.

Trading For Beginners

www.ingramcontent.com/pod-product-compliance
Lightning Source LLC
Chambersburg PA
CBHW071053240526
45471CB00015B/1833